WOMAN POWER

TRANSFORM

YOUR MAN,

YOUR MARRIAGE,

YOUR LIFE

WOMAN

POWER

THE COMPANION BOOK TO

The Proper Care and Feeding of Husbands

Dr. Laura C. Schlessinger

HarperCollins*Publishers*

HarperCollins books may be purchased for educational, business, or sales promotional use. For information, please write: Special Markets Department, HarperCollins Publishers Inc., 10 East 53rd Street, New York, NY 10022.

FIRST EDITION

Printed on acid-free paper

Library of Congress Cataloging-in-Publication Data is available upon request.

ISBN 0-06-075323-4

04 05 06 07 08   ❖/RRD   10 9 8 7 6 5 4 3 2 1

For family, friends, colleagues, and fans who have stood by me—in humble gratitude.

Acknowledgments

Without the sensitive, honest, open, generous, and profound contributions of my audience—this book wouldn't have been possible. Thank you for helping me help others.

It's a funny business, a woman's career. The things you drop on your way up the ladder, so you can move faster. You forget you'll need them again when you go back to being a woman. That's one career all females have in common—whether we like it or not—being a woman.

Sooner or later we've all got to work at it, no matter what other careers we've had or wanted . . . and, in the last analysis, nothing is any good unless you can look up just before dinner or turn around in bed—and there he is. Without that, you're not a woman. You're something with a French Provincial office or a book full of clippings—but you're not a woman.

—BETTE DAVIS, in the classic film *All About Eve*

Contents

Author's Note

Consider this companion book your personal companion, as you take an important journey. I promised with *The Proper Care and Feeding of Husbands* that "if you buy the book, read it, and do what it suggests—you will be happier that you're married . . . and to him, within forty-eight hours." Sounded cheeky even to me! Then came the hundreds of letters that testified to the change having taken place within minutes or hours. That is because *The Proper Care* was not about awkward actions like greeting your man at the door in plastic wrap—it was about a change in heart, mind, spirit, and attitude. Although they may joke to the contrary, men are really not very interested in daily raunchy seductions; they are desirous of daily warmth, appreciation, and affection. Inanimate objects are not required.

The Proper Care was also not, in spite of feminist reviews/tantrums to the contrary, about making women submissive, servile, opinionless, or weak. Quite the opposite, and that is why this book is titled *Woman Power*. As one male listener, a college professor, wrote:

> *"We are each blessed with different moral powers. In some instances, these moral powers divide nicely along gender lines; in others, it is simply a matter of natural gifts. Giving is not about rendering oneself servile. Rather, it is about standing tall and*

using one's moral powers to enrich the moment. It is the exercise of our moral powers in this way—be it between husband and wife, or parents and children, or one human being and another—that so marvelously and wondrously sets us apart from the lower animals."

What has, throughout all time, been special about women is their natural tendency to bond, nurture, nest, show compassion, and love. When we speak of "mother love," we talk about the purest and strongest of all affections. When we speak of "mother's milk," we talk about the medium through which life itself is transferred. Women are special creatures with the ability (together with a husband and God) to create life within their wombs. Mothers are the source of life and sustenance, through breast-feeding and emotional caretaking. Through social bonding, women are the link between their men and family and society. Through their acceptance of a particular man, women are a powerful force in determining the social behavior of their men (if bad boys couldn't get a woman, they would give more thought to being good boys).

This naturally results in *woman power.* As adults, men come to women, in part, as a boy comes to his mother, generally not in any neurotic way but as the natural journey of a man. He lives for the same approval and appreciation and affection and attention he yearned for from his mother. And when he does get that from "his woman," he is better able to conquer the world, and will be completely devoted to her.

When women "get it" and "use it," their men, their marriages, their lives are transformed. And even in the midst of financial woes, illnesses, recalcitrant children, annoying neighbors, and a dog that won't be house-trained, both wife and husband are happy.

Woman Power is part standard book, part journal, part workbook, and *all* a positive way to take the basic concepts from *The Proper Care* and expand and reinforce those ideas to help you transform your life, and that of your family, into the spiritually sound and satisfying experience it could be.

Introduction

While this book stands on its own in inviting and guiding women to maximize their inherent potential for transforming their men and their marriages into experiences of joy and satisfaction, it is also a response to the many questions from both husbands and wives, generated by its "sister book," *The Proper Care and Feeding of Husbands.*

In that book I pointed out that, as Cathy Young wrote in her review of it in the *Boston Globe,* "In the age of feminism . . . we have paid a lot of attention to women's complaints about men and criticized men for not meeting women's needs—but we've forgotten that men too have needs and women too have faults. Somehow, we've even developed the notion that a woman who seeks to meet her husband's needs is subservient (but a husband who fails to meet his wife's needs is a pig). . . .

"Part of the problem is that feminism . . . offers very little by way of an alternative. Too often (Schlessinger is right about that), it has promoted anger, rancor, and male-blaming instead of equal partnership. The majority of women do want loving relationships with men."

Amen to that! I have found it fascinating that most women are really not all that aware of how dismissive they are toward their husbands and their husbands' needs. That mentality has become so commonplace in our culture that most women don't register it as unkind, thoughtless, cruel, abusive, or down-right mean. But it can be. The almost-universally positive re-sponse from women who have actually read the book has been immensely gratifying to me. Instead of a knee-jerk defensive-ness based on the mistaken notion that they are being blamed for all the world's ills, women have embraced the concept I have offered them: that, as women they have the power to transform their men, their marriages, their homes, and their lives into a more positive, rewarding experience.

Here is one all-too-typical example of a wife not under-standing her power. I recently took an interesting call from a second-marriage mother and her eighteen-year-old daughter. The daughter felt helpless to deal with her mother's overt jeal-ousy and resentment that her new husband of three years was paying more kind attention to the daughter than the mother.

Of course, I immediately pursued the possibility that this guy was hitting on the daughter. Nope. I checked with the mother to find out if the daughter was being seductive with the stepfather. Nope. I then asked the daughter to hang up the phone, promising her that her mom and I would deal with it.

I admonished the mom for putting her daughter in the middle of her own marital problems. Then we got into some details. The mom had three complaints: that he was cheerful when the daughter called him at work but short-shrifty when she called him; that he was cheerful with the daughter when he walked through the door at the end of the day but did not have that same greeting for her; that he was cheerful when the daughter requested a favor but wouldn't do what she asked of him no matter how often she nagged about it.

"My dear," I queried, "when you call your husband at work is it to whisper sweet nothings or naughties into his ear? Or is it to whine or nag him about something?"

The latter.

"When your husband comes home, do you greet him at the door with a cheery 'Hi honey, glad you're home, kiss, kiss'?"

Nope.

"When you ask him to do something for you, do you pick it apart afterwards or show gratitude?"

The former.

"Then what do you expect from him with all this negative training? I just want to know what happened to catching flies with honey?"

I explained to her that when the daughter called him, greeted him, appreciated him, it was a more positive experience than when she, the wife, engaged him. Simple as that. This goes along with part of my thesis, that men are simple—not simpletons—but simple in their needs—i.e., not complex. They need appreciation, approval, and affection from their woman; and when they get that, they will, as I've said many times on my radio program, swim through shark-infested water to bring us lemonade.

Women wield more power in man-woman relationships. Men are born of women, raised by women, and come to women for their bonding and mating. Throughout their whole lives, women are central to men's emotional well-being. I don't think we can come up with one story about a man committing suicide over the breakup with a golf buddy. We all are aware of the devastation that can be wrought by a man's frustration when he is not loved, admired, appreciated, and embraced by his woman. That hurt, rejection, or loss can virtually end his motivation for life. Most men live to serve their wives and children—their families. When they are not made to feel that they are appreciated for those efforts, they become hurt, lost, lonely, and not very cooperative.

Within only two weeks of the publication of *The Proper Care and Feeding of Husbands,* I received a letter from a six-foot-four, two-hundred-and-fifteen-pound police officer. It was painful to read, but I shared it on my radio program. The response to it from all across the United States and Canada was amazing. Why? This big, masculine, powerful, accomplished guy was turning into depressive mush because his wife never seemed to be proud of, or happy with, him. This letter registered with men and women alike. Men from all walks of life identified with his pain. They, too, in spite of loving their wives, were starting to imagine a life without them.

The women identified, in whatever small or large part, with his wife—and were overwhelmed with sadness and regret. All during the two weeks after this reading, hundreds of wives wrote to me that, after having a good cry, they all contacted their husbands at work and told them that they loved them and were proud of them. They all also reported that their husbands seemed transformed into happier human beings, offering to help with this and that without being asked!

Simple. Took five minutes . . . tops.

I have never been asked for more copies of anything else I have read on this program in thirty years! That letter triggered hundreds of letters from women who did what Jeanah, one of my listeners, did within minutes of hearing me read Robert's letter. She faxed me this:

> *"I feel that a 'thank you' is not enough to say to you and the gentleman who wrote the letter you just read. I fear that I am one of those women.*
>
> *"I have been sitting at my desk listening on my headphones in my regular working stupor. That letter stopped me dead in my tracks.*
>
> *"I just ordered a bouquet of flowers and chocolate to be delivered to my husband at work. The card reads, 'I am proud to have you as my husband.'*
>
> *"I'm leaving for the rest of the day, to buy something sheer and frilly. When he comes home, I'll be on the bed, wearing not much, holding grapes and a cheese ball. I'll keep the remaining details to myself.*
>
> *"See you on the happier side of marriage."*

The Proper Care and Feeding of Husbands gave articulation to the pain that men feel when the woman for whom they are willing to do anything does not idolize them. It is not that most women or wives are mean. It is that women have not been encouraged to understand and appreciate men and masculinity. Women have been trained to see men as "the evil empire" and to perceive giving as subjugation. Sad.

Unfortunately, there were also letters from men whose wives refused to read the book. That very refusal was experienced as a personal rejection of the men who wondered aloud why she wouldn't want to know more about their feelings and needs. Dave, a listener, wrote:

> *"My wife has seen me reading it and knows about the book, but she has not asked me anything about it. I don't know if this is because she doesn't want to look in the mirror or if it is the typical disinterest in what I am doing. I am sure many men have this same question. Since the hope is to improve the situation, you don't want to appear as though you are making a threat or giving an ultimatum. But you also want to make it clear that you identify with the men and situations in the book."*

I hadn't quite anticipated how this book would resonate with men and how they would embrace it. There is so little in our culture that respects men and masculine thought, feeling, and behavior. I suppose that, to some extent, *The Proper Care and Feeding of Husbands* filled that vacuum. Still, it is sad to imagine men who are actually frightened about the potential backlash from their wives when they present them with that book.

David, a listener, wrote:

> *"I bought* The Proper Care and Feeding of Husbands *because I wanted to read it myself just to see if I had unrealistic expectations of my wife of seventeen years. I spent several hours reading the book cover-to-cover several times and was amazed to see virtually every page was dead-on on some aspect of my marriage. I am going to try to get my wife to read it.*
>
> *"It is unreal what simple creatures men really are. If I could just get that little bit of physical love from my wife, I would absolutely be her slave. I have told her this many times and it is just so much water off a duck's back. I work sometimes twelve*

to fourteen hours a day to provide the income necessary for our family to live with some degree of comfort. And all I ask from my wife is fifteen minutes a couple of days a week (which I never get). She doesn't seem to understand what damage is done by this lack of attention. I have tried to explain it to her with no success. If I can get her to read the book, I am sure that your words will help ease the frustration and pain."

I can appreciate the defensiveness many basically decent women might feel when handed the book by their husbands. It is uncomfortable to be confronted with the knowledge that one has been rather insensitive or self-centered. However, there must also be the relief that comes with (a) knowing the problem and (b) knowing that YOU have the power to change most everything for the better.

Valerie's letter expresses this sentiment beautifully:

"OK, I give in. I've been thinking about reading your book for a while now, but I kept thinking, 'But what if he still doesn't help me out if I do all this attitude change for him?' It seemed so unfair!

"Well, I was listening to your interview on KSFO this morning. You were talking about a big, burly policeman who felt bad because his wife never said she was proud of him. You said that, after you had read his letter on your show, a bunch of wives called their husbands to say just that, that they were proud of them. You also talked about how moody women are. You said all this after I totally went emotional, moody, and loony on my husband last night. I won't even tell you what it was about, it's just that embarrassing to me now.

"So, I called my husband after that and said, 'I realize how nutty I was being last night, and I'm really sorry. Thank you for being such a good husband.'

"He then said, 'I respect you more than I respect myself, I'd kill for you, your life means more to me than my own.'

"I still tear up when I think about that. Talk about my emotional needs being met! I have suddenly forgotten what

housework I wanted him to do. He just made me feel like the only woman on earth today. I am sooo off to the bookstore today to buy your book. If saying something that 'small' to my husband encouraged him to say something so 'big,' you must know what you're talking about."

Simple. Five minutes . . . tops.
And ladies, don't wait until it's too late.
A listener from Yucaipa, California, wrote:

"I'm sitting here crying after hearing the caller with two young children and a husband who is not 'happy' for no reason other than his age. I, too, was not satisfied with a man who was kind, gentle, handsome, hard worker, trying to make me happy. He was a great father and he worked at the job he loved.

"I thought I should have more attention, he should have a better job (we covered the bills, but not a lot extra), and that I could find a man who was better if I wanted.

"I didn't tell him I appreciated all he did and all he was.

"Today, a year after he died at forty-nine of cancer, I cry for all my son and I have lost. Today I would tell him how much I loved, needed, appreciated him, twenty times a day if it would make him happy. I know that he was the greatest guy in the world.

"I wish with all my heart that I had a second chance; that your book and words of wisdom came sooner rather than too late."

And now the second form of too late—which is only sometimes fixable.
A man from North Carolina wrote:

"I am writing today to give the other side to this wonderful new trend caused by your new book, The Proper Care and Feeding of Husbands. *I am a husband who has now been separated for over a year. During the two years of my marriage, my wife would refer to me as stupid or pathetic, or say that she should*

have married someone else. I would tell her how much that hurt me, and she would say that I was a baby and that I was not a strong enough man if I could not take her words and occasional slaps.

"I remember feeling worthless and useless most of the time. I never did get her to understand what that did to me. I eventually became afraid to tell her anything that I was feeling. The hardest thing that I ever did was to tell her to leave. Men love to feel as though they can protect their wives from the dragons of the world. But I have learned that my wife had more power to destroy me than anything else I could have faced. For my marriage, your book is too late."

It is dispiriting to report that I've gotten many letters like this one from men who are defeated, destroyed, and demoralized simply by not feeling cared about by their wives. Another husband wrote:

"The total sense of rejection that accumulated over time as a husband, father, friend, and lover—I could do nothing right—affected every part of my life, including, ultimately, my ability to provide financially for her and our four children. After our fourth child was born (she wanted a fourth), she slowly pushed me aside sexually over the next four years. At the point when we had had no physical contact whatsoever for two months, I told her how rejected I was feeling and that I was having a hard time concentrating at work because of it. Her reply was a snapping, 'Get used to it!' Tears came to my eyes. I asked her for quiet time together on the sofa to talk and hold hands. Her reply was, as she walked away, 'I haven't got time for that.' "

And don't think that the psychotherapeutic environment has been any less hostile to husbands. Generally, psychotherapists are ideologically liberal, drenched in the feminist anti-male mentality which is propagandized in most of their training programs. Therefore, when husbands push for marital counseling, hoping the therapist will help them reach their wives, they too often find themselves with cannons to the right of them, cannons to the left of them.

The following excerpt represents all too typical experiences for men in couples' counseling:

"After finishing [The Proper Care and Feeding of Husbands]*, I begged my wife to read it. She reluctantly agreed.*

"After reading [it] my wife looked at me with scorn. She asked how could I ever give her anything that questioned her as a wife and that I was completely insensitive. I explained that it was not meant to be perceived negatively, but rather just to give her a view of how men see relationships. She immediately said, 'We are going to couples' therapy!'

"A week later I found myself in front of a therapist who chastised me for wanting simple things like a hug, kiss, an 'I love you,' and god forbid . . . sex. The therapist said my wife had no obligation to give me these things, and my demanding them was a source of control in which I intended to strip her of her power.

"I could not believe it! Then came the stake in the heart. My wife told the therapist that I actually had the nerve to give her your book to teach her how to be a good wife. The therapist immediately rolled her eyes and said, 'That book has made women think they should submit to their husbands and take on a subservient role. I would toss it in the fireplace.'

"I write you this letter not only to vent, but also to warn your readers about the resistance they may face with some therapists and counselors. Make sure your therapist wants to encourage a healthy partnership for you and your spouse, and not just spread the common belief that the woman is always the victim."

Men are starting to come out of the closet and admit that they are hurt and angry and don't want to take it anymore. Tim, a reader, called my radio program asking me what he should do with his anger toward women, an anger crystallized by reading *The Proper Care and Feeding of Husbands*!

He said, "I've just been reading your book and it's brought

up a lot of anger in me and I just don't know how to deal with that. I walked out on my nine-year marriage some four years ago. The women in your book are just like my ex-wife. And it's just brought back nightmares. I fell in love with my wife when I first met her and it was the happiest day of my life. And by the time I walked out the door, I was just like an empty shell of a man. And, it's as if she had ripped every bit of manhood away from me by the time it was over. I'm very jaded, very cynical, I guess, towards women now. I don't know what to do with that anger."

The Proper Care and Feeding of Husbands has validated the perspectives and feelings of a lot of husbands who, frankly, have felt disdained, mistreated, or even psychologically and emotionally abused by their wives. I do tell them, however, that holding onto that anger is poisonous to their well-being and life satisfaction, and they should take note of the kind of personality and mind-set they would prefer in their future relationships. (I recommend my *Ten Stupid Things Men Do to Mess Up Their Lives.*)

It's obvious that we women wield tremendous power over our relationships with our men. It's obvious that our men can be motivated to greatness in and out of the home with the smallest words and gestures of love, admiration, and support from us, their wives. It is also obvious that what we have the power to give we have the power to take away. We should not take that power lightly. We should not take the needs of our men lightly.

Perhaps one of the most compelling letters that deals with this issue of what a husband really needs came recently from an ex-prostitute. Wow! What a perspective. Melissa wrote that she stripped by day and sold her body at night from the age of sixteen.

"There is a misconception that all hookers are on street corners and that all 'johns' are degenerate, perverted, dirty old men looking to indulge in sick acts that their prim and proper wives at home won't do. Though this is the case sometimes, I am compelled to tell you another side.

"The majority of my clients were married, but the truth is that at least 90 percent of them NEVER TOUCHED ME. They would pay me to do acts their wives wouldn't do . . . but it was things like LISTEN, fix them a drink, light their cigarettes, and stroke their egos . . . pay attention to them and make them feel good—but I'm not talking sexually.

"You would be shocked at how little actual sex I had with clients, and I'm including Clinton's definition of sex as well. These men had to pay money to get from someone else what they weren't getting at home. I always thought how incredibly sad they were, and even though they were married, how alone they always came across."

Imagine. The men were going to a prostitute to get what they weren't getting at home: attention, approval, appreciation, and affection. Sex was incidental. The men's true needs were met by a woman paid to just listen and be kind.

As Bob, a listener, summarized:

"Dr. Laura, keep on spreading the word about men's feelings, and the simple needs we have. As much as women crave to be 'Queen Bee' in the home, husbands need to be treated as something special, too . . . before it is too late!"

None of this is meant to condemn or blame women for all the ills of the world and the home. All of this is meant to affirm that women have almost magical powers to create the atmosphere in their homes in which their own joy and pleasure, as well as that of their husband and children, flourish. And it isn't complicated—although difficult at first to break old habits and be vulnerable. No tools or assembly required. Just a look of the eye, the tone of a voice, the touch of a hand.

Simple. A few minutes each day . . . tops.

—*Dr. Laura Schlessinger*
FEBRUARY 2003

WOMAN POWER

PART ONE
Yeah, But . . . What If?

Questions and Challenges About
The Proper Care and Feeding
of Husbands

For some, the titles *Proper Care and Feeding of Husbands* and *Woman Power* are provocative and controversial—especially side by side.

The former title strikes some as one-sided, hostile to women, 1950s retro, dangerous to women's civil rights, and an affront to already-hardworking women who see any request or desire from their husbands as selfish and oppressive.

The latter title strikes some as the war cry of feminists ("I am woman, hear me roar" or "These boots are made for walking and that's just what they'll do; one of these days these boots are gonna walk all over you"), one-sided, hostile to men, 1960s retro, dangerous to children's rights, and an affront to already hardworking men who see their wives treat any request or desire as selfish and oppressive.

This just goes to show you that it's all perspective and attitude. The "feminist" notion of woman power as a rejection of femininity, of child-rearing, of loving a man, and of maintaining a home both for physical and emotional comforts has robbed women of choice and satisfaction. One female radio talk show host thanked me at the end of the interview about *The Proper Care and Feeding of Husbands,* by saying, "You've made caring about your man acceptable again."

The ultimate power of women is their unique qualities: intuition, compassion, nurturance, sensitivity, sensuality, bonding, and nesting. Women throughout the ages have been the ones to center men (the emotional safety and warmth of home and hearth, acceptance of him), give men purpose (providing for and protecting wife, children, and home), control male aggressive and promiscuous urges (the civilizing impact of responsibility to family and children). Women are also the ones who ultimately create the atmosphere in the home.

It saddens me, as a woman and as a communicator to millions of men, women, and children each day, that women have been indoctrinated to see that as subservience rather than power.

But since these issues, sadly, are controversial, many questions arise; some in your own mind, and some to handle when you are challenged when others less enlightened see that you're reading this book! Here are the most frequently asked questions and challenges since I published *The Proper Care and Feeding of Husbands.*

This is also the beginning of the "interactive" part of this book. After each Q & A, there is a space left for your reactions, thoughts, challenges, feelings, notes, reflections, admissions, and commitment to growth or change. You don't have to take these questions in any particular order.

Also, you may wish to use these questions as points of discussion with your husband and/or your book club or women's group, or with a friend with whom you are taking this journey as "study buddies."

Question 1:
How do I know the difference between a bad man and a "hungry" man?

"I have a concern regarding your new book, The Proper Care and Feeding of Husbands. *Women who are involved in hateful, abusive relationships may take the advice you give and try even harder to make a potentially fatal relationship work, taking on the guilt that the fault for the abuse is on them for not trying hard enough to please. Maybe you could let the thousands of women who are in these relationships know that there is a possibility that your wonderful book may not be helpful in a relationship that is abusive mentally, emotionally, and physically. Thanks for all you do for all who will pick the wax out of their ears and their egos and listen to you."*

I couldn't agree more! That is why on the first page of *The Proper Care,* in the "Author's Note," it reads: "As I pointed out in my first book, *Ten Stupid Things Women Do to Mess Up Their Lives,* and reiterated in *Ten Stupid Things Couples Do to Mess Up Their Relationships,* the 3 A's: Addictions, Abuse, and Affairs, are behaviors, in my opinion, that break the covenant and justify the self-preserving decision to end the relationship. Where the behavior of one or both of the spouses is blatantly destructive, dangerous, or evil, this book does not apply."

That said, there are some ramifications of this idea of a "bad man" that I think need attention. Since the release of *The Proper Care and Feeding of Husbands,* many women have written to me that even though their men have had affairs, or were drinking too hard or working too long, or were just not being cooperative around the house or perpetually displaying a negative attitude, that their own attitudes toward their husbands after reading the book had the power to heal and redirect them both. I never, never, never blame one person for the choice of behavior or actions of another. I always, always, always make it clear that people must take responsibility for their own actions in spite of whatever influences or pressures they may be experiencing from others.

However, it is a fact of life that many people make bad choices because of those influences or pressures. It is also a fact that unhappy men often make stupid, destructive choices because of those influences or pressures. It is a fact that most unhappy men are unhappy because their souls, psyches, and hearts are not being attended to at home, by the only people with the power to transform them—their wives.

Men are more directly dependent on the acceptance and love from their wives for their general well-being, than vice versa. Women get that kind of support and feedback from their mothers, sisters, friends, hairdressers, manicurists, etc. As when they were children, men turn only to their women (mommies and then girlfriends and then wives) for the human touch. Remember the end of the Sylvester Stallone movie *Rocky*? When Rocky beat the champ, bleeding yet triumphant, the only thing he called out was the name of his wife, "Adrian!!!" Same thing happened in the Cuba Gooding Jr. and Tom Cruise movie *Jerry Maguire*. The hero cried and threw kisses and love into the camera for his wife. Football players say "Hi Mom!" on camera during a game. For men, the acceptance, appreciation, attention, and affection of their wives is oxygen, a warm blanket, adrenaline, safety, purpose, and even the ultimate meaning of their lives.

Some of the women whose husbands strayed or started working too many hours outside the home took responsibility for not having created a home atmosphere that made home a magnet for their men. Their letters did not read like those you might expect from panicked, dependent women. Their letters did read like those you would expect from mature women, bravely acknowledging that they'd contributed to an atmosphere that created tensions in their men, setting the scene for their husbands' bad choices. They admitted to rejecting their husbands' sexual and loving advances, to rarely asking for their husband's input with respect to children, not spending time listening to them or considering their issues important, and so forth.

What these women discovered is that the majority of the power in the man–woman relationship is held by the woman, because of a man's natural emotional and psychological dependence on her. This *is not* about *fault*. This *is* about *power.* Now, does that mean men are wussy wimps? No, of course not. The same man who will crumble at the criticism from his woman, could run into a burning building to save the lives of complete strangers.

Any woman who thinks for a minute that this is subservience is way off track in her thinking, and handicapped in her ability to have a fabulous marriage. As Lori, a listener, wrote:

> *"I have been called 'oppressed' by a man by my feminist sister and family members. I'm told I don't 'need' a man to take care of me, I shouldn't 'waste my brain,' etc. Over time, I have come to realize that putting the care of my husband and son first, has, in a way, freed me to grow as a woman and a human being like nothing else could do."*

Whatever happened to "it is more blessed to give than to receive"?

One new bride of four months didn't have any trouble with "giving," she had trouble with the hostility of other women caused by her being so giving to her husband.

> *"My husband and I entered our relationship with the benefit of having seen that the action of love is a choice that is made DAILY. My husband constantly tells his friends that he has the best wife in the world (although I am not). He fills my life with joy. As a new bride, I have learned that my husband enjoys having his lunch packed for him every day. Recently, a woman at my church stopped me in the hallway and said to me, 'Honey . . . we DON'T fix their lunches every day . . .' and*

then laughed. Although I know what she said was a 'joke,' it carried the implication that I have much to learn as a wife. I couldn't help but think that SHE was really the one with something to learn. I don't do those things because he demands them or because I am 'the little wife,' I do them because I love him, and I want him to carry that knowledge throughout his day, his week, and his lifetime."

In response to me reading this last letter on my radio program, one husband wrote:

"My response to the new bride: 'Don't let anyone stop you from showing your love and appreciation for what he does for you and how he responds to your feelings.' I've heard unhappy people give ridiculous advice like that to young brides, and I know they are bitter people who just want company on their hate train."

Finally, what some women call abusive or controlling sometimes gets silly. Sometimes it seems that many women are so down on men, they harbor the notion that even some minor input from him is oppressive. Yikes.

One young man called my program recently with his fiancée, unbeknownst to me until the end of the call, sitting right there listening to every word he was saying. He called because his fiancée wanted to call off the wedding but still wanted a relationship with him.

For the life of me, I couldn't get a handle on what the problem was. When that happens, I trust my instinct that there is more to the story than I'm hearing. It was when I challenged him ("What are you holding back?") that he said "she" was sitting right there. Clearly, he was afraid to tell the truth in front of her. Sad. And not very promising for a marriage.

I terminated the call because I could not help him when he wasn't free to express himself. The problem? Her mother and she have decided he was controlling and have given him the following examples: (1) when she is two to three hours late to a date with him, he is being overreacting and controlling to request that she leave a message or give him forewarning or apologize to him once it has happened; (2) two months after proposing to her, he had to go away for a month for work-training. His fiancée's mother said that she should be able to go out with guys as long as there was no sex. She did go out a few times with some guy, got drunk, and had him stay overnight with her. The mother and the fiancée said that his trying to call off the wedding at this point (because he felt she was not ready for a committed relationship) was disrespectful to her, overre-active, and, again, controlling.

Sadly, when all of this seems so ridiculous and obvious, he asked, "Should I try to salvage this relationship? Am I being controlling? Should I let her continue to use me by maintaining the relationship that she wants to have with me? Am I stupid? How do I replenish my self-esteem after something so damaging? They have made me feel as though I am the scum of the earth. I feel as though they are simply trying to beat me down to a helpless emotional state."

For too many women, anything a guy says, wants, or needs is controlling. Those are not going to be happily married women.

Your turn:

_____

_____

_____

_____

_____

_____

_____

_____

_____

_____

Questions 2 and 3:
How do I undo years of the lack of proper care and feeding? And why should I be the first one to change?

"I recently finished reading your new book, The Proper Care and Feeding of Husbands, *and was very pleased with it. However, I feel that you did not emphasize two issues enough: (1) if a woman has been mistreating her husband for fifteen, twenty, twenty-five, or more years, can she realistically expect that all will be right in a day or two? (2) women, as all of us have a tendency to do, will often say, 'Why should I be the first one to change? I'll change when he changes!'"*

With respect to the first part of the question, frankly, I did not expect that either women or their men would change as quickly as they did. It was only after receiving hundreds of faxes within days of the release of *The Proper Care,* that I realized the true magnitude of the enthusiasm and hunger of the women to have some immediate, powerful tool to transform their marriages into happier experiences, and the immediate, enthusiastic adaptability of the men. I began reading these "testimonials" on my radio program to inspire others, only to geometrically increase the responses testifying to the immediacy of a "change."

Based on this feedback, I began "promising" that "If you buy this book, read it, and do what it tells you, within forty-eight hours you will be happier that you're married . . . and to him." I didn't promise this to sell books. I could promise this only because the readers told me it was so, and I am committed to helping couples have more loving, satisfying marriages.

Here is, happily, a typical example. One listener wrote:

> *"I hate to admit it, but somewhere along the line I became one of those pain-in-the-butt wives you have been talking about on air and in your new book. I realized I have been taking my husband for granted. What didn't dawn on me until Monday, when I heard you talking about your book, was that I needed an attitude adjustment toward him. I continued listening on Tuesday and Wednesday. I heard you talk about wives so caught up in the 'me and my needs' garbage . . . and they sounded like me! I ordered your book immediately, and sent my husband an e-mail yesterday.*

(Here is the e-mail she sent her husband.)

> *"I am having one of those really emotional days today. I think I have come to an epiphany on my part about you and me. I'm sorry. I wanted to take the time to say that to you, because I don't know if I have said it enough. I would like to tell you why. I'm sorry for not realizing that you needed me near you more, I'm sorry for volunteering outside my home when I could have volunteered more often to help you and to love you. I'm sorry for thinking that I had to save the world but I forgot where and who the world was . . . it was in my home, lying next to me. . . . it was you and I forgot to save you. I'm sorry for overly criticizing you at times and for not hearing you out. I'm sorry for not just holding your hand and stroking your cheek more. I'm sorry that I didn't realize that I was working my way toward*

losing you and not working my way toward you. I apologize in advance for the days I may lose sight of what is important to me. Please help me to keep 'us' and 'our family' in the forefront of my mind."

"When I came home he had tears in his eyes and told me he loved me very much and would do anything for me and that he was so grateful to know that I still loved him. Last night we talked honestly and tenderly for the first time in many years. His face seemed younger and he smiled more than I can ever remember.

"This morning before the kids got up I took the time to tell him 'Thank you'—a statement that was long overdue and needed. He wanted to know 'What for?' I told him, 'For putting up with me and for being such a good man.' This morning he held my hand and walked me to my car when I left for work, even offered to make me lunch and take me to work."

Another listener wrote about how quickly things turned around in her marriage:

"I've been married for sixteen years, and I've been very unhappy during the last ten years. We have no children. I prayed and prayed that God would help heal our marriage, and nothing seemed to improve. I blamed everything on my husband. Then I hit rock bottom two weeks ago. I even got mad at God.

"We had a big fight over something stupid. But words were said and I was very hurt. I went into my normal silent treatment for four days. On Sunday, my husband informed me that he wouldn't go to church because he didn't want to kiss me during the sign of peace. Ouch! Did that hurt. After church, I went to walk through some stores. For no special reason I was drawn to Barnes and Noble.

"I walked in the door and guess what was staring right in my face?!!! A standup picture of you and your new book. I saw the title and became teary-eyed—thinking, 'Why not? I have nothing to lose by reading this.' I went home, closed the bed-

room door, and read the entire book over the next three evenings. Everything was making sense, everything was clicking, and it sank in. I realized what I had been doing. I wasn't being nice to my husband—I was treating strangers better. I stopped the nagging. I started to be more loving and kinder.

"I took all your words to heart, and by the finish of the book (third evening), let's just say I was enjoying every single moment of it!! And it's true—just like you said: my husband is doing things for me now that he never did before. I don't even have to ask—he wants to please me because I'm making him happy, too. This is incredible—all we're doing is being nice and kind to another! I know we'll still have some shaky times ahead . . . but now that we are kinder to one another—I'm sure it will all work out for the best."

During a radio interview for *The Proper Care,* a caller asked, "You said, Dr. Laura, that if I do the stuff in your book, that my husband will start being nice to me. Well, what if I do this stuff, you know, act nicer and all, and he doesn't trust it and keeps waiting for the other shoe to fall. You know, what if he feels like it's just a manipulation or nothing that will last?"

Before I could speak, the male host said, "Madam, if you meet him at the door, all loving and seductive, he isn't going to spend one second analyzing motivations or anything else."

Men are very hungry for our love and very receptive when fed. Don't worry 'bout that.

Question 3 is mostly explained in question 2. However, to be pointed and succinct: we women should do "it" first because we have more power to transform our men than they have to transform us. That's the simple truth. Women have the power in relationships with basically decent men. "Ain't nobody happy 'less momma's happy," is a universal fact of life. Men shift emotional gears more easily, are more dependent on our moods than we are on theirs, marinate in negatives and minutia of relationships less, forgive more readily, are less complicated, let things go more quickly, and are simpler in their emotional needs than we are.

All in all, that gives WOMEN the POWER! Why would any woman not want to know that *she* has the power to almost immediately transform her man, her marriage, and her life? The power is awesome. When it is used benevolently, sensitively, and intelligently, just about any wife can make any husband the happy, loving, "die for us" kind of guy he wants to be. Try it. You'll like it.

Your turn:

_____

_____

_____

_____

_____

_____

_____

_____

_____

_____

_____

_____

_____

_____

_____

_____

_____

_____

_____

_____

_____

_____

_____

_____

_____

Question 4:
How do you maintain the changes?

"I realized months ago that I was causing problems between my husband of forty-one years and myself. As you spoke about the book last year before its release, I knew I needed to buy it and read it. I found it a week ago and have studied it for the last week. With pencil in hand, I realized I was underlining a good deal of the information. I have turned the book jacket to the wrong side so it wouldn't be obvious to my husband what I am reading. I need to STUDY the information and don't want him to be distracted. I would rather he notice a difference in me.

"Within a couple of days, my husband said, 'You have been more loving.' It brought tears to my eyes. I still haven't told him about the book, because I have a long way to go. I have found that old habits die hard. Self-centeredness and thoughtlessness have become automatic. The chapter about sex was totally enlightening. Imagine, I have been married to the same man for forty-one years and never understood his needs. He is a fine man, hardworking and patient. I know he loves me and I hope to be a better wife and companion. Bless you. I have the book in my purse so I can reread and review.

"But my question is, how do you maintain the changes and not go back to old habits?"

First of all, give yourself a break. Changes do not ever occur all at once or in a straight line. Old habits are sometimes hard to break. The real test of learning and growth is not perfection (not possible), but the acknowledgment of that lapsing back to oneself with an apology to the other person (very possible).

Secondly, the same way old habits are maintained, new habits are created. Habits stay in place because they are familiar and there are benefits. Bad habits have benefits simply because the familiarity breeds comfort and there are perceived "gains." For example, let's look at turning down your husband's sexual advances. It may just seem easier to do that than to bathe and primp, wonder about his reaction to your cellulite, designing a life less stressful than the harried state you're usually in by nightfall, having to bother yourself with his satisfaction, letting him think for a minute that you have let go of that anger you had about . . . whatever, and so forth.

Now, the new habit: Responding to your husband's advances and even making a few of your own will make you feel more relaxed about life (orgasms do have that effect); you feel more womanly and sensual; you feel closer to your man; daily annoyances in general, much less those having to do with your husband, seem to have less importance; and your husband seems not to be able to do enough for you . . . to name only a few "gains."

These positive aspects help reinforce your new behaviors. Please, worry less about how good you are going to be at it, and enjoy more the peaceful and more satisfying life and marriage you'll have because of it.

So, think small and steady. Do one or two small things differently during the first few days, then add small things a day or so later. You may be thinking that you'll feel a bit exposed, vulnerable, or just weird if you change some of the ways you behave. If you do, that's normal and OK. However, I bet that your changes will make you feel so good that those uncomfortable feelings will be short-lived.

Your turn:

_____

_____

_____

_____

_____

_____

_____

_____

_____

_____

_____

_____

_____
_____
_____
_____
_____
_____
_____
_____
_____
_____
_____
_____

Question 5:
Are there "typical" things about wives that
drive men nuts?

"What are the most common complaints men have about their wives?"

Men are hurt that their wives:

- Don't seem to have much regard for their feelings and needs.
- Constantly criticize and dismiss them.
- Don't want to go out of their way to please them.
- Nag, demand, and complain—and seem to behave as though they were *entitled* to do so.
- Don't make them feel truly needed and valued as *men*.
- Don't make a priority out of making the home "homey."
- Don't treat them with respect.
- Won't read *The Proper Care and Feeding of Husbands*—which men interpret as their wives not caring enough

about them to learn about their needs and respond to them. The husbands who have written me about their wives' refusal to read the book also interpret this resistance as a basic selfish hostility.

"Avid Fan," a listener, wrote:

"Before heading home, I stopped and purchased your new book and wrote my bride a letter that if she was interested in having a happy and loving home, to read the book. She has been warned by her meddling and seemingly man-hating mother about the evil and sinister Dr. Laura. I have no idea if she is reading it or has thrown it in a round file. I guess I will have to wait and see if the very basic need of acceptance will start to show up or my bride will disappear.

"By the way, I just discovered a couple of books she is reading in her private time that you may know about: Ditch That Jerk *and* Inside the Mind of the Angry and Controlling Man. *"*

(More about the antimale messages in our culture later in this book.)

Another fellow wrote in to say:

"When I told my wife I had bought your book and wanted her to read it, she just laughed at me. You don't know how much that hurt me. I could not sleep that night at all. I just lay awake in bed thinking how much my wife didn't care how I feel. That pain doesn't go away."

Another male listener, sharing that pain, wrote:

"Women seem to have no idea how they are hurting themselves and us by being so constantly judgmental. Not only are they missing the key to entering their mate's true heart and soul, they are, in fact, killing both. God bless you for writing this book. My wife will never read it, I'm sure. She was angry that

I bought it for myself. As a result, she will continue living in her world by herself, thinking only of my faults, shutting me off, and isolating herself at the same time. I have a new understanding that I'm not defective, not alone."

These sentiments were universally expressed in the letters from the men. I had no idea that the dissatisfaction, dismay, and downright unhappiness was quite as great as it is in America's husbands. The misery of married men has clearly been a well-kept secret, based on the typical response of women listeners. They would fax in after I read one of those sad letters from men, expressing compassion . . . and surprise. They never thought . . . and that's been the problem.

One male listener wrote:

"I have not read a book, except technical manuals, since high school. Well, I could not put yours down until I finished every bit of it. Reading your book made me nod my head constantly, stare away in thought repeatedly, and cry a couple of times in reading some parts that were my life—described by strangers. I have experienced a lot of the hurt and rejection explained in many chapters of your book. No, my wife is not that terrible! Your book made me realize that she may not even know she is doing some of the things I consider hurtful. It summarized my hurt by category, it surmised my feelings by chapter, and angered me even more with each page. No, I do not mean to criticize your book. I got angry in reading about all the things that I am going through, through someone else's life, calls, and comments.

"Angry that I was reading the book, those same problems were growing even bigger, that communication with my wife was getting sparser, that sex with the woman I love with all my heart and soul was just another chore to her.

"She has been trying to feminize me since we got married, and it is exactly because of this women's movement and her friends' influence (almost all of them divorced) and television program garbage about what a woman should be and what a man's role should be.

"Thank you, Dr. Laura, I will give her your book tonight. If she is the woman I know her to be it will change our lives. It might take a little time to reverse the brainwashing she has been subjected to her whole life, but I feel this is the ice breaker."

By the way, he signed the letter: "Just Another Man in Love With His Wife." Believe it or not, not one of the "complaint" letters, really "plaintive" letters, said otherwise. Like faithful dogs, for goodness sake, these men love us no matter how little they get from us. That's one of the realities that makes it easy for wives to *unilaterally* "turn the tide" in their homes from cold and combative to warm and mushy.

But before we women get to feeling too inappropriately confident, the men also express the following sentiment: They may "love" us, but they don't always "like" us. Hence, forgetting the anniversary or birthday.

Actually, most acts of "forgetfulness" are intentional. Consider this letter I received the day before Valentine's Day:

"I am halfway through your book and am blown away that you understand me better than I did. However, even though I would never even in a million years consider divorce, I am plagued by that little thought and notion that I am worth more than this and deserve better.

"I came home last night and did everything I could to please my woman, my wife, but at the end of the night, after I had cleaned the dining room and the kids' room, got the kids ready for bed, did the dishes, talked about both—no, not both— just her busy day, I was ultimately rejected yet another time, because her world was not picture-perfect and she was just not in the mood.

"Consequently, on my way out the door today, I gave the kids a kiss and told everyone good-bye. I noticed a not-very-nice look on my wife's face. I said, 'What's wrong, honey?' Then she said, 'Aren't you going to kiss me before you leave?' I told her, 'You'll deserve a kiss when I deserve some physical intimacy with the woman I call my wife.'

"She gave me a nasty look.

"Dr. Laura, I am so frustrated I want to bang my head against a concrete wall, and what's worse is all she can do is talk about what we're doing for Valentine's Day—I say, screw Valentine's Day!"

I believe that many women do not intentionally aim to hurt their husbands. I see though, that too many wives are oblivious to the fact that much of the way they behave decidedly hurts their husbands. It is my contention that women have been so incredibly negatively brainwashed with respect to their roles and relationship with men, that they, indeed, do not see their obligations, only their own defensive concerns. Women are most concerned with making sure they are fulfilling what society has told them should be their only role: money + acquisition + position + independence = POWER. They've been told that without that power they will be oppressed, servile, meaningless, used, and useless. Obviously, this notion of POWER does not include doting on a home, husband, or children. This notion of POWER makes women power-LESS to achieve really deep satisfaction in their personal lives.

Your turn:

_____

_____

_____

_____

_____

_____

_____

_____

_____

_____

_____

_____

_____

_____

_____

_____

_____

_____

_____

_____

_____

_____

Question 6:
What do men want to be fed?

"What are men's most important needs?"

Men want their wives to:

- Need them.
- Admire them.
- Desire them.
- Respect the fact that to feel like a man he needs to provide for and protect his family.
- Show approval, appreciation, and affection.
- Not make them feel like being "male" or acting "masculine" is tantamount to being deformed.
- Respond to physical contact and affection for feeling of connectedness and love (no, ladies, they aren't just "horny bastards").

I dealt with this issue with a woman who called, overwhelmed with her lifestyle and wanting to know how she can get her husband to stop annoying her about sex.

"I like sex OK, it's just that he is always trying to get some."

"Always? How often do you have sex?"

"Oh, I don't know, couple of times a month or so. But he is always bugging me about it."

"Let's try this. I am going to ask you one question. You are not to answer me in any way. Let's see what happens between us."

I then asked her what time it was—that's all. When she didn't answer, I got repetitive, more impatient, and louder while trying to elicit a response.

"What happened here?" I asked her.

"I get it. When you get no response it builds up a determination and a desperation to get something back."

"Bingo! If you were to seduce him . . . he'd stop nagging. If you were to be lovingly responsive to his 'come on,' . . . he'd stop nagging. You, believe it or not, are stimulating the nagging by your rejection. You have the power to make the nagging go away. He doesn't want 'it' all the time, no matter what the jokes are about men never getting enough. He wants you to want him. When he feels wanted 'that way,' he will be less compulsive about trying to get it from you. Don't you see? He needs you—that's what the sex is about—having *you!*

Another of my male listeners wrote:

"Do you know why most husbands die before their wives do? Because they WANT to! I have been a major contributor in my chosen profession, and am known nationwide, having been president of a 25,000-member professional organization. I have awards, plaques, and certifications that would fill a room. I have spoken in over thirty-five states . . . and to my wife, it was still never enough or good enough. I would have given it all up just to hear a soft, comfortable word, or any type of recognition from that one person who meant the most to me, my wife."

I can't repeat enough times that, with respect to their emotional well-being, men are quite simple in their needs. If you still don't believe that's true, try this simple test: approach your man when he's not in his best mood. Put your hands on either side of his face. Gently kiss the tip of his nose and both cheeks. Tell him that you think he is "quite a magnificent man." Watch what happens to his eyes. Then you'll know.

Your turn:

_____

_____

_____

_____

_____

_____

_____

_____

_____

_____

_____

_____

_____

_____

_____

_____

_____

_____

_____

_____

_____

_____

_____

_____

Question 7:
Does "simple" mean "stupid"?

"Isn't calling men 'simple' an insult?"

Not at all! In fact, almost all of the many hundreds of responses I received from men in preparing *The Proper Care* confirmed just that. Men are not emotionally complicated. Men are fairly consistent in attitude and temperament. Men focus on the concrete. Men do not spend time ruminating over the tone with which their wives made one comment. Men do not overanalyze events, actions, and words—unless they are getting paid for it. Men are not overly sensitive. Men are quite practical, not emotional.

Think about it. When was the last time you heard a story about a difficult father-in-law? When was the last time you heard of a father- and son-in-law having at each other?

I remember when my son was in first grade. I thought, "What a great question!" I asked my boy what was the difference between how girls fight and how boys fight. I will never forget his answer: "Well, Mom, when girls get mad at each other, they get other girls to be mad with them, and stay mad forever. When boys get mad at each other, they yell and shove, then they forget about it and go play ball."

That's what I mean about men being "simple." Your basic, decent man is actually quite easy to get along with. Maybe that's why they are so easily taken for granted.

Please take time to think about how simple your man's needs are, how they are centered around your appreciation, approval, and respect, and how you might make more of a point of attending to those needs. Take some time to think exclusively about your husband.

My concern is that not too many women have put much effort into that latter activity. At a recent book-signing, when married couples came up together, I would ask the wife to tell me one thing that was wonderful about her husband. About 85 percent of the women came up with something nice im-

mediately. To the man, each had tears in his eyes almost immediately; tears and big grins.

The leftover 15 percent either stumbled about or came up
with something generic, like "He plays golf, swims, and runs."
To the man, each had tears in his eyes almost immediately;
tears and no grin.

It was sad and embarrassing to see. I don't think the wives
were consciously trying to humiliate or disappoint their husbands. I truly believe that they just never spent any time thinking about what was good about their men.

Your turn:

Question 8:
Is there something I can do to make my attitude more positive?

"What is the No. 1 worst mistake women make with respect to being happy in their marriages?"

They marinate in negatives. Unfortunately, it is more typical of women to fester and ferment over disappointments, slights, annoyances, angers, etc. Women, more typically than men, will go over the "bad thing" ad infinitum in their own heads with their mothers, sisters, friends, coworkers, neighbors, social groups—even book clubs! In doing so they reinforce the negative and create and perpetuate a bad attitude—one which turns into entitlement to not being particularly nice.

A female listener wrote:

"I have been terrible to him with my attitude—always bitching about something, never happy with anything he does or says, always focusing on what he doesn't do or say. Listening to you has opened my eyes—thank you."

Your turn:

_____

_____

_____

_____

_____

_____

_____

_____

_____

_____

_____

_____

_____

_____
_____
_____
_____
_____
_____
_____
_____
_____
_____
_____
_____
_____

Question 9:
Why is "attitude" so important?

"What do you mean about having the right attitude?"

"Attitude" is about believing that your mate has your best interests at heart—and returning that favor. It is *not* about letting loving feelings and actions be squelched by everyday annoyances and disappointments. It is about giving the benefit of the doubt. It is about cherishing the moments and living for the well-being of the other, and being sustained by the joy of giving and the blessing of receiving in return.

Your turn:

_____
_____
_____
_____
_____
_____
_____

_____

_____

_____

_____

_____

_____

_____

_____

_____

_____

_____

_____

_____

_____

_____

_____

_____

_____

Question 10:
Why pick on the women?

"Why did you write this book aiming at the women—aren't both husband and wife responsible for the quality of the marriage?"

Of course! I do believe, though, that with respect to relationships, women are the natural leaders.

If you've ever been to a farm, you'll know that water pumps generally need priming. And to prime a pump, you use water. When the priming with water is done properly, water gushes forth. Women are the primers, the men are the pumps. Instead of competing and measuring, women should accept their power to transform their men, their marriages, and their lives.

A very smart wife wrote:

"I now know that the toxic feminist message of 'We are created to be equal to men' is so damaging and contradictory. God loves us equally, but he created us differently. He created us to help and edify each other, and to be a team."

Your turn:

_____

_____

_____

_____

_____

_____

_____

_____

_____

_____

_____

_____

_____

_____

_____

_____

_____

_____

_____

_____

_____

_____

_____

_____

_____

Question 11:
Well, what are the guys supposed to do for us?

"Are you, Dr. Laura, going to write the book for men on the proper care and feeding of wives?"

Nope—frankly, I don't see it as necessary. Men spend their entire lives in the tutelage of women. The horrible problem is the lessons they've been learning from all of these women. From too many mothers who sacrificed them to institutionalized daycare or nannies because of a career, they learned they weren't really important. From women who would abort their babies because . . . they felt like it and could . . . they learned they weren't really important. From women who would get pregnant and not marry the "fathers" and deny those men access to their babies, they learned they weren't really important. From women who go to sperm donors and raise children on their own, they learned they weren't really important. From wives who cater to their mothers' opinions over their husbands', they learned they weren't really important. From girlfriends who would shack up and have sex without a covenant, they learned that being a man had nothing to do with honor and responsibility, and was, instead, all about fun.

Men are learning every day . . . the question is, are those lessons good for women, men, children, or society?

We women have to take responsibility for how we raise our sons as well as how we present "womanhood" to the men in our lives. When, for example, "nice girls didn't," boys were clear that there were lofty values and ideals to aim high for. When men were expected to support their families, they worked hard to qualify for the hand of a good woman.

If you want your man to work toward something with you, be the lofty goal. If you, for example, want him to work hard for the family, tell him how grateful you are to know you can count on him. Watch *him* roar!

Your turn:

_____

_____

_____

_____

_____

_____

_____

_____

_____

_____

_____

_____

_____

_____

_____

_____

_____

_____

_____

_____

_____

_____

_____

_____

Question 12:
What, I don't have enough responsibilities as a wife?

"Isn't having the POWER actually a burden for women?"

Interesting way to look at power. I see it just completely the opposite way! Women are burdened by a society that demands that they be independent, successful, powerful, and not burdened by children, a husband, and a home. As the *New York Times Magazine* (surprise!) pointed out in November 2003, high-powered, powerful, successful women were giving it all up, because the deeper meaning of their lives and more profound fulfillment came from home, hearth, kids, and a husband. The true *nature* of a *woman* is to *nurture;* that should not be denied. When women are burdened by the pain, hopelessness, and helplessness of a failing marriage and family . . . that is the ultimate burden.

I am trying to help women see that they are indeed very powerful influences in the quality of their lives and marriages. Women are unique in that ability. Families throughout the ages resonate to the frequency produced by the woman of the home. What women accept or reject gives a clear message to men about the boundaries of their behaviors if they wish to enjoy that affection and awe from their women. I am reaffirming the power of women to transform men, their families, and their lives. That power is not a burden—it is a blessing.

I believe that within families and relationships, women are the natural leaders. The ideas and techniques in *The Proper Care* are simple and sweet. What a blessing for women to know that they largely control their own happiness. My job is to get their prejudices out of their own way. Transforming your guy into a loving man is its own reward!

Your turn:

_____

_____

_____

_____

_____

_____

_____

_____

_____
_____
_____
_____
_____
_____
_____
_____
_____
_____
_____
_____
_____
_____
_____
_____

Question 13:
Where was I when they gave out the owner's manual for husbands?

"Have women always misunderstood men so extensively?"

No. There was a time, in our grandparents' generation, that men were not seen as the evil empire, the source of a woman's misery and lack of accomplishment and happiness. Mothers would teach their daughters about "male ego" and "feminine wiles" so that they would be better able to navigate their journey through marriage and children. Catering to a man was not seen as diminishing the woman, no more than catering to a woman was or is perceived by men as diminishing the man. It was universally perceived as the loving thing to do.

Times have changed—but the needs of men and women, and the realities of the masculine-feminine polarity, do not change. I now have newly married women calling about "a dilemma" that has occurred since they have been offered a great job four states away from their husband.

"Shouldn't I be maximizing my potential? Shouldn't he be willing to let me do this if he loves me? Should I be letting my husband decide my future? Am I supposed to give up my dreams?" are the all-too-typical questions today. Because of the heavy influence of "rights" of women, many women are confused about having to make adult choices (and understand that means foregoing something else) and don't understand that vows, commitment, honor, and good will are as important as, if not more than, a promotion. Unfortunately, this attitude seems to show itself even with regards to minor, dependent children. So much for liberating women from their responsibilities for the sake of their "potential."

Does that mean that I don't believe women should have dreams, careers, jobs, hobbies, etc.? Are you kidding? Look at me! However, I am the poster child for squeezing in all your dreams around your loving obligation to your family.

When "we" are married, it is no longer about "me," it is about "us."

Your turn:

_____

_____

_____

_____

_____

_____

_____

_____

_____

_____

_____

_____

_____
_____
_____
_____
_____
_____
_____
_____
_____
_____
_____
_____

Question 14:
Oh, aren't men just all about sex, sex, sex?

"What is wives' worst misconception about masculinity?"

That a man's sexual needs for his wife are purely physical; that may be so in his fantasies and with nonwives, but with his wife it represents her love, connectedness, acceptance, and his desirability to her. When he is rejected continuously, his self-esteem, happiness, and even desire to live are damaged.

Don't believe me? Read this:

> *"I had tears running down my cheeks when I heard you talk about your book about caring for husbands on your program. I have had to endure this for over twenty-five years. I don't believe my wife has initiated sex more than twenty-five times in the last thirty-five years. We have been married for over fifty years. I have not been physically touched, kissed, a kind word, or had sex in at least fifteen years. So much for marriage. I don't know what I can do. I am seventy-five now and have lost all of these years. I'm old and bitter, with tears in my eyes as I write this to you. Please do not use my name because I am so ashamed."*

He is ashamed for fulfilling his marital obligations in spite of being treated as an incidental by his wife? His wife should be ashamed. I wonder how many of you women are married to this man?

Your turn:

_____

_____

_____

_____

_____

_____

_____

_____

_____

_____

_____

_____

_____

_____

_____

_____

_____

_____

_____

_____

_____

_____

_____

_____

Question 15:
If I make more money than he does, am I "the man"?

"How can a wife make a husband feel like the provider and protector if she is working, too, making the same or more money than her husband?"

Marriages in which the woman dominates in "outside power" (money and position) have an inherent fragility. In this situation, women more often feel superior and dismissive of their husbands. However, when the man earns more or all, the superior and dismissive attitude is less likely to exist, because men have always taken *pride* in providing for their families, not *disdain*. Of course, with the so-called changing times, men have been taught that they are no longer responsible for "providing"—this has led to an alarming tendency of many men to threaten their wives with divorce when the women decide it is better for the family if they stay home and raise the children. Chilling—but it goes to show you how women's liberation liberated men from a sense of definition of manhood and, with it, a sense of personal, moral, and social responsibility.

One former at-home mom with just such a "role-reversal" situation precipitated by her husband's layoff wrote:

"I am now working full-time and operating my business out of our home. It had only been a few weeks, and I found myself feeling the pressure and stress of being the primary source of financial support for the family.

"It was like a light went on in my head, and I thought . . . wow! This is how he feels every day of every week of every month. I have been given a glimpse into my husband's mind that I am extremely thankful for, because I think that when he does go back to work I will understand things about him like . . . how I like to come home and just enjoy my child without worrying about helping to clean the house, and I like not to have to go to the grocery store to pick something up on the way

*home and worry about making dinner, or if there will be any-
thing to eat when I get home.*

*"When I get home at night and he meets me at the door
with baby in hand, giving me a kiss, and the house is reason-
ably clean and so is the baby, I feel like I can stop being the
'dragon slayer' and I can start being a wife and a mother. I want
to remember this and give him a home that he loves to come
back to with less for him to worry about and more hot food on
the table.*

"In the midst of all of this I read The Proper Care. *What
a unique perspective I had while reading this. I am thinking
about myself taking care of him like I should, and then thinking about how I like to be taken care of when the roles are re-
versed. I really think that 'walking a mile in his shoes,' as cliché
as that sounds, has helped me to understand some of my husband's emotions and needs. I don't know many who would
admit it, but I really think that men need to feel safe and accepted in their homes and by their wives in order for them to be
good husbands and fathers."*

Yes! That is exactly my point. We women, our Women
Power, is what civilizes and transforms men from "males" to
husbands and fathers.

Women who decide to stay in the competitive workforce
need to make sure that they find ways to permit the sense of
"provider and protector" to be experienced by their husbands,
and enjoyed by themselves. For example, have your husband
take care of the finances; never throw your money in his face;
make sure to show positive interest in his endeavors; ask him
for concrete suggestions with your work; even though you
have your own income, find ways to show him his contribution is important to you and the family.

Frankly, though, I still think too many women bought into
the feminist ideal of a woman burning her candle at both ends
with having it all at once: work, school, home, motherhood,
and marriage. I still contend that when a woman loses the

connection to her femininity, and the protection and succor of her man, that she loses too much in her life and takes too much away from his.

Your turn:

Question 16:
Aren't you idealizing men a bit too much?

"You recently remarked on your radio program that there is abuse of men by women. You were talking about the T-shirts being sold, which say 'Boys Are Stupid,' and about women who aren't nice to their husbands. While I find that type of attitude distasteful, I also think that you sometimes seem very one-sided on this issue—especially now that your book is out . . . which I have already purchased and love.

"I am not a raging feminist. I am a twenty-five-year-old black woman, and consider myself to be reality-oriented. While two wrongs don't make a right, the rage that some women feel toward men is not completely unjustified. A lot of men are really disrespectful toward women in general. Many have a really in-depth, intense disregard for women. The superiority complex that many of them have seems almost innate, and extremely obvious. I love men, and appreciate them greatly, but they don't seem to find women interesting unless they are related to them or have a work or love interest. As we're growing up we're taught to accept that that's how men are and that we have to develop loving attitudes regardless of how we've been treated. (By the way, I have a wonderful boyfriend who would 'swim through shark-infested waters to buy me a lemonade.')"

That some men are jerks (and so, by the way, are some women) is a point I drill home in my first book, *Ten Stupid Things Women Do to Mess Up Their Lives*. Obviously, and as I point out in *The Proper Care*, those are not the guys to bring home.

That men do not spend much time on women they're not married to, dating, related to, or working with . . . is a criticism? Men are very task-oriented, and their relationships generally have to have a "point." No woman should take it personally. To "hang," guys generally go to their guy friends. But then again, don't we do that?

Your turn:

Question 17:
Don't nice guys finish last?

"Why is it that some women will do the proper care and feeding of jerks? How can women expend copious sweat and tears on abusive men, yet give a good one table scraps of affection and attention? What is a man to do in this situation?"

Women who waste time and life on jerks are not psychologically healthy in the first place. Those relationships take the place of growing up, taking on responsibility, facing internal conflicts, running away from fears or problems, burying oneself in the drama of the moment, and so forth. They often find themselves with "good guys," but are so confused, damaged, or afraid that they undermine those relationships because they "know" that they "don't know" how to be in a healthy relationship. They usually abort the potentially healthy relationship by finding fault with the "good" guy, which they don't seem to mind as much in the "bad" guy.

As I pointed out in my book *Ten Stupid Things Men Do to Mess Up Their Lives,* when a man decides to rescue the damsel from the dragon, and the dragon is herself, he just ends up with a distressed damsel—usually for life. If he can't motivate her to get the help she needs to help herself, he should run far away and fast.

Your turn:

_____

_____

_____

_____

_____

_____

_____

_____

_____
_____
_____
_____
_____
_____
_____
_____
_____
_____
_____
_____
_____
_____
_____
_____
_____
_____

Question 18:
What's going to keep men from using this book to "get without giving"?

"For a troubled husband who has a wife who neglects him the way you describe, this book is a lifesaver. Are you concerned that some might use it as a battering ram against their wives? If so, what do you recommend?"

I might have worried about that before I got feedback from the thousands of men who are basically frightened to death to approach their wives with the book. The single most frequent question from the men was, "How do I get my wife to read the book without her getting even more mad than she usually is with me?" How sad is that?!

If, however, this is the case, I recommend that the wife agree to read it with her husband so that they can talk about each point together—even if she has to do it under the guise of wanting his personal feedback on the points of the book. The book clearly points out, in letters from the men, that the men are transformed . . . so, he'll have to transform if he so believes in the book! The basic behavior of reading it together turns it into a "we" and not a "her."

I have only gotten one call (this is true, not a joke) from a woman describing this problem: "He has always been verbally and psychologically abusive to me. Now that he's read your book, he's using that for more ammunition."

"Madam, why have you stayed with an abusive man?"

"I am on oxygen, with last-stage emphysema."

"Then, learn to ignore him."

What else could I say?

Your turn:

_____

_____

_____

_____

_____

Question 19:
I don't have a spouse. What's in this book for me?

"Is this book relevant to unmarried folks?"

Most definitely. I believe it is important to have an understanding of male/female issues as one develops into an adult
looking for a quality relationship. Both men and women need
to know what is healthy and reasonable to expect, and what
kinds of behaviors ought to be rejected, along with that individual, if necessary.

Your turn:

_____

_____

_____

_____

_____

_____

_____

_____

_____

_____

_____

_____

_____

_____

_____

_____

_____

_____

_____

_____

_____

Question 20:
Even your title is anti-PC!

"What made you decide to write this book in the first place?"

This book is written in response to repeated calls to the show from husbands who were feeling just tortured by their wives' indifference and unforgiving behavior, and calls from wives who lost touch with why they married in the first place, who were treating their husbands so outrageously . . . and didn't seem to realize it, or accept it when I brought it to their attention.

Just recently a woman called about getting her daughter's ears pierced. Her husband was "fer" it and she was "agin" it. That in and of itself intrigued me. It seemed backwards. When I asked her why she was against it, she said it was because they would be imposing this on a child who wasn't old enough to make up her own mind and might have a problem with it when she was older.

"Are you kidding? A girl have a problem with jewelry? What is really going on?"

I pressed and pressed. Until she finally came out with the truth.

"My mother said it was a bad idea and I shouldn't do it."

"Let me get this straight. Before your mother's comments, did you have a problem with it?"

"No, not really."

"Are you somewhat afraid of how your mother would respond if you went and did it anyway?"

"Yeah, I guess so."

"But you have no fear of how your husband would respond when you tell him 'No'?"

"Yeah, I do."

"Really?"

"No, not really, I guess."

"So here it is, you are intimidated by your mother, and because of that you are willing to disrespect your husband and his opinions and feelings in his own home, with his own wife, about his own daughter. How could you do that?"

It took several go-arounds before she "got it."

It is not that she, or most women/wives for that matter, are bad people. It is that most women have been blinded to caring about what their men think, feel, and want. They are more closely tied into their mothers, girlfriends, and women's magazines—most of which dismiss men as a necessary evil.

Your turn:

_____

_____

_____

_____

_____

_____

_____

_____

_____

_____

_____

_____

_____

_____

_____

_____

_____

_____

_____

_____

_____

_____

_____

_____

_____

Question 21:
Am I supposed to be an unpaid prostitute on demand?

"Why should I have to have sex when he wants it and I'm not in the mood? Why should I be obligated to having sex just because he wants it?"

The issue of sexual intimacy is probably one of the most contentious problems in marriages. Being distracted now and then by stresses, illnesses, problems, exhaustion, emotional pain, and so forth, is a normal, natural, understandable part of life.

Playing the "I'm not in the mood game," or giving into the laziness and ennui that comes with being self-focused is not a normal, natural, understandable, or acceptable part of a married life.

Women call me with all sorts of excuses about not wanting to have sex; many are reasonable excuses. But so what? It still all results in (a) damaging, hurtful rejection of a husband, (b) loss of opportunities for stress relief, (c) loss of opportunities for reenergizing the relationship with extreme pleasure, (d) husband–wife disconnect, (e) husbands feeling unnecessary except for paychecks and oil checks, (e) less interest in sex as time "without" marches on.

One recent woman caller complained that her husband just wasn't understanding enough about how busy, tired, stressed, hormonal, etc., she was. Her question for me was, "How do I get him to stop nagging me about sex?"

I reminded her that sex was part of the covenant and asked her if she told him at the altar that he was only going to have two or three years of sex for the rest of his life . . . unless, of course, *she* felt like it.

I asked her what importance she thought her husband felt in their home?

I also asked her how she would feel if every time she touched him he slapped down her hand and said, "Not now. I'm not in the mood."

I told her that the less she engaged in intimacy with him, the thicker the wall would become as it became less familiar and, therefore, less comfortable.

It seemed as though she was gaining some understanding and sympathy for his feelings.

"Oh my, I didn't think of it all that way. But should I have sex just to please him even if I'm not in the mood? What should I do?"

"If you don't feel like feeding the children, do you starve them? If you don't feel like being nice to your mother when she calls, are you a bitch to her? There are zillions of things you do each day because you are responsible, considerate, thoughtful, and sensitive. Why do your husband's emotional and physical needs for you not fall under the same umbrella?"

"Do I just lie there?"

"My dear, if you are not in the mood to be pleasured, you can still show your love for him by pleasuring him. There are lots of things you can do for him . . . and you'll probably get turned on in the process more times than not. I've gotten too many letters from husbands feeling like they love their wives but are staying for the children and living in painful, emotional isolation, because they are at the insensitive mercy of their wives' 'moods.' Don't let your marriage become one of those.

"And isn't it true that we are only 'in the mood' if our day has been perfect and he hasn't done any picayune thing to annoy us? Isn't that the truth?"

"Yes," she admitted, "it is. Thank you."

The very next caller said she was struck by the truth in that conversation, and recognized herself ignoring her man's needs because of her "moods." She reported that she had just called her husband at work, in the middle of a meeting, to tell him, "When you come home tonight, no matter how tired I feel, how messy the house is, how bugged I am by anything, we are going to have some fun!"

She said he got very excited.

Another female listener sent me a fax the very next day about "faking it."

"I've finished your book, passed it on to several friends, and we all thank you. I've heard many callers in the past few weeks ask you about 'faking it' with their husbands. Well, here's my perspective. If a husband and wife love each other, they are willing to act in a way that is not keeping with their emotions once in a while—what many people call 'faking it.'

"My husband has faked it many times, and I am always grateful. When? When I've arranged a social outing that he's not really that interested in. But he knows it means something to me, so he puts on a smile, holds his arm out for me to wrap mine around, and fakes it. When? When I've got something on my mind that he can't relate to, but that I want to get off my chest and air my feelings in a safe, nongossip environment. So he strokes my hand and lets me ramble for twenty minutes until I'm 'all better.' He doesn't necessarily understand all I'm reacting to—but he fakes it. When? When he comes home from a hard day and I can tell he's exhausted and discouraged, has nothing left to give, and would prefer nothing more than to be alone for a while. But our beautiful children come bounding down the stairs calling, 'Daddy's home!' And he puts aside every bad feeling, turns on the smile, digs down to find some

energy from his reserve tank, and showers those kids with hugs and kisses. He really isn't feeling happy or energetic, but they don't ever know that, because he 'fakes it' for their sake.

"My point? Though his actions can be described as 'faking it,' because it's not his feeling at that moment, that very act of 'faking it' proves that his love is always real—never, ever faked. 'Faking it' is really putting your love *before your* mood.*"*

Your turn:

_____

_____

_____

_____

_____

_____

_____

_____

_____

_____

_____

_____

_____

_____

_____

_____

_____

_____

_____

_____

_____

_____

_____

Question 22:
Once we get the idea—then what?

"If we wives now 'get it,' where do we go from here? What do we need to do, think about, change, deal with, and so forth? What are some tips, directions, advice, and support to help us properly care for our men and get the most out of them, our marriages and our lives?"

The rest of this book is geared to answer all those questions. Enjoy the journey.

Your turn: If you have any question you don't feel has been answered in this part, please xerox this page, writing that question on this page, and fax to Dr. Laura Schlessinger at 818-461-5104 for a brief personal or group answer. Please include your return fax number.

PART TWO

Proper Caring:
"Was It Good For You?"

Assessing Yourself and Your Marriage

Before we get to a specific list of questions for you to use to think more deeply about the quality of your marriage, I believe it is important to focus on where answering these marital-assessment questions will take you. In thinking about bringing positive changes to your life and your marriage, I would like you to always remember the two A's: *attitude* and *action*. When in private practice, and now on my radio program, I have learned that most people think their attitude must change first, and that action will follow naturally. While that can happen, it is not the rule. More important, we may all get old together waiting for an attitude change. Life is happening now. Without a change in actions *right now,* ships can be sunk—and so can marriages.

Responding to what she thought was an appropriate assessment of her young marriage, Bonnie, a twenty-four-year-old caller to my radio program, performed an action that could have ruined the lives of three people: Bonnie's husband of six months, her eleven-month-old child, and herself.

BONNIE: I'm calling because I have recently admitted to my husband that I am no longer in love with him.

DR. LAURA: Oh, gee, that was a great thing to do.

BONNIE: Well, it was the truth.

DR. LAURA: Bonnie, people often do damaging things and justify it by saying, "It's the truth." There are certain things which, when said, cannot be taken back.

BONNIE: Yeah, I understand that.

DR. LAURA: So, you're a woman with a small child who has just blown up her kid's home. Smart. How do you know when you're in love? How does Bonnie know when she is in love?

BONNIE: When I think about the person during the day; when I'm happy to see them; when I miss them when I'm not around them. You know, the infatuation part.

DR. LAURA: That's not love. You got pregnant by him and now you want to blow him out of the water of his wife and child?

BONNIE: Yeah.

DR. LAURA: Really nice, Bonnie.

BONNIE (crying): I admit that it was selfish to tell him that. I'm lucky that he still is willing to pursue a relationship and is still very much in love with me.

DR. LAURA: I have an assignment for you. You are going to do four things each day that you imagine a woman in love with her husband would do. Then we will talk again in two days. OK?

BONNIE: OK.

Bonnie did call back in two days.

BONNIE: I had called your show the other day because I had been rolling over and over in my mind an incident that had happened a couple of days prior. I had been talking with my husband, and we had a lot of issues: raising our eleven-month-old child; we're both full-time students; we have opposite schedules so we don't get to see each other very much; we got pregnant early in our relationship and got married; we didn't have much of a honeymoon period because of all these responsibilities. I think that honeymoon period is something that people are always trying to get back in their relationship. And I felt like I lost that. I wasn't feeling physically attractive and I was turning down his proposals for making love. And, I just guess I started reminiscing back to prior relationships in high school that were infatuation-based. I always thought that a couple in love or in a marriage would always retain that emotional passion—that infatuation.

I've done a lot of soul-searching since we talked. I starting reading your book and talked openly with my husband about what I had done and what you told me to do. I wrote down a list of things that a woman in love would actively do in her marriage. At first it wasn't easy for me to do, but once I started I realized that I haven't been doing the things I should be doing. What I did was selfish. I was hurting and I just needed to give that hurt to somebody else. I see how that is destructive and I know that I hurt him. He has forgiven me. I was really immature in thinking that a mature relationship is going to be comprised mainly of feelings of infatuation.

When I asked her if she "did" the four things a woman in love would do for her man, she replied that she had "thought" about what those things were, but didn't actually "do" them. I gave her two more days to take care of that part of the assignment. Two days later:

BONNIE: Well, I wrote down a list. It was really embarrassing, because it was so hard for me even to start, because you were making me think of things that someone would actually *do* instead of being such an emotional reactor. I finally did start a list of some things I thought I would do if I felt like I was in love with my husband. One of the first things I would do was tell him, "I love you." I think I had kind of stopped doing it as much as I used to. So, I started doing that again.

Our relationship right now is strained, because of the fact that we're both full-time students and we have a little boy that we take care of full-time. He's not in daycare. He's either with my husband or me. But we are two ships passing in the night. I haven't made my marriage a priority, and it was selfish of me to confront him the way I did. I understand why I did it. It was just a stress reliever for me. When I talked to you and actually realized what I had done it scared me to death. I've never had a relationship past the lovey-dovey stuff. Even with my parents, I haven't had a comfortable kind of love with them. And I think that's what a marriage is really about.

The rest of the list is making love, then making sacrifices, and then doing things specifically that are of interest to him even if they're not necessarily of interest to me.

DR. LAURA: And, you can't be both going to school at the same time. You see, you two agreed to get married, not be roommates with a kid while you both went on with the goals of your single lives.

BONNIE: Yeah, we started completely backwards.

DR. LAURA: One of you needs to be home and uncrazed, or else you're not going to have much of a life together. That's probably the biggest sacrifice people have to make when married; they have to give up their single lives.

As Bonnie and I talked, it was clear that she learned the lesson that loving feelings are generated by loving actions. A good attitude about marriage comes from the actions that put a priority on that marriage. Actions beget attitude. Actions and attitude beget happiness.

Your turn:

_____

_____

_____

_____

_____

_____

_____

_____

_____

_____

_____

_____

_____

_____

_____

It is also true that really paying attention to the actions and attitudes of your partner can make you happier that you're married, and to him. A listener faxed me about a seemingly small occurrence in her life—however, one which literally woke her up! She wrote that she has been married for six years, with two children under four. She admitted that since she had children, her relationship with her sincere, loving, giving man who would do anything for them, had not been a priority to her.

The very day she started reading *The Proper Care and Feeding of Husbands,* was the night that her *husband* came from work to meet her at their daughter's preschool open house.

She had volunteered, along with fifteen other mothers, to make cookies for the event. She continued:

> *"When my husband arrived, there were at least fifteen different types of cookies out on the table for us to choose from. He walked over to me, gave me a kiss hello, and asked which cookies I had brought. I pointed to the chocolate-chip cookies, which looked boring, compared to all the other fancy cookies—in fact, they hadn't been touched yet.*
>
> *"I watched him pick up a plate and grab two of my cookies. When he sat down, I asked him why he took my cookies, which he always gets at home, instead of trying something new? He answered simply, 'Because you made them.' It dawned on me right there what your book is about. My husband is all about loyalty to me and his family and making us feel good. I realized what a simple creature my husband is, I was touched by his loyalty, and thought about how easy he was to please. I, on the other hand, tended to complicate even the smallest things.*
>
> *"Right there, I patted him and thanked him for choosing my cookies. And he answered, 'Of course I would. You are my wife.'*
>
> *Thank you for setting me straight on appreciating the most important man in my life, my husband!"*

Your turn:

_____
_____
_____
_____
_____
_____
_____
_____
_____
_____

_____

_____

_____

Another listener sent me a letter titled: "Hallelujah! I've had a revelation."

> "I've just finished reading your book. I was getting ready for work when my cat came up and wanted attention. I immediately stopped what I was doing to pet and talk to her. While I was stroking her, she flopped over on her side and started purring with happiness. While I was telling my cat how beautiful she was and how much I loved her and enjoyed her company, I realized that while I stroke my cat's ego, I have been failing to stroke my husband's ego! I've learned from your book that I need to give my husband at least the same attention I give my cat.
>
> "From this day forward, I will shower him with affection, and although I doubt he will purr out loud, I know he will become more content and loving in return."

Your turn:

Now, I need you to forgive what will seem like a detour from the concepts of *attitude* and *action*. I believe that the first attitude change we women need to assess and, if necessary, effect, is the attitude women have developed about themselves as women. Without a lovely, appropriate assessment of the status of "woman," it is a lot harder for wives to reconcile their issues as wives and mothers.

The morning I was thinking about this concept, an unusual thing happened. I was having breakfast in my hotel room, after an out-of-town book-signing, when I decided to flip on the television for some R & R. The television turned on to a classic "true story" about a minister, Peter Marshall, titled *A Man Called Peter,* set in the late nineteen-thirties, early nineteen-forties. The young woman the main character eventually marries is the only one of three students courageous enough to stand up and talk to a rowdy assembled group of teenage and early-adult couples about temperance. What she said absolutely floored me in its simplicity and beauty.

The girls in the crowd were boisterous, drinking, smoking, swearing and laughing with approval at their boyfriends' boorish behavior toward the minister. She began by saying that she believed that the boys they were with didn't really like their behavior, and that sonnets have never been written about women because they smoked, drank, swore, were promiscuous, boisterous, or rude. She added that this behavior also did not bring out the best in their men, which didn't result in the best for society.

I almost fell out of my chair. Support for the very issue I had been thinking about only minutes before was coming from a film made almost fifty years ago?

As a Christian woman, she told them that the first serious declaration of woman's majesty and liberation came from Mary being chosen as the mother of the savior of the world. She said that this elevation of woman was to a height greater than men, and lamented that it was so sad that to these young girls "women's liberation" was behavior that copied the worst behavior of men.

I then opened up the *New York Times* and, as if an exclamation point to that experience, read an *un*critical cover story on women becoming entrepreneurs in the porn industry, where the profiled female pornographers described their endeavors as selling "female empowerment." "Female empowerment" is how we describe the degradation of our sexuality?

I reflected upon my childhood perceptions of being a woman. Those things sweet and mysterious, gentle and loving, sensitive and vulnerable were the cornerstones of what I thought I had to look forward to. I imagined a man adoring me and protecting me.

Then came the feminist movement, which took all that away and put in its place an aggressive sense of entitlement, anger, suspicion, self-centeredness, insensitivity to anything male, and disdain for anything historically feminine. To get married and become a mother was, to these activists, to lose their identities. And replace them with what?

We gave up too much of what is unique, lovely, and satisfying to ourselves as women and appealing to our men.

This, then, is the place to start with your assessment of your marital relationship. We start with your assessment of your womanhood/feminity.

What is singular in importance to you about being a woman?

_____

_____

_____

_____

_____

_____

_____

_____

_____

_____

_____

How has the above changed throughout your life?

_____

_____

_____

_____

_____

_____

_____

_____

_____

_____

How has the feminist movement impacted you positively and negatively?

_____

_____

_____

_____

_____

_____

_____

_____

_____

_____

How does your past and current (if different) opinion about the "place of a woman" impacted your relationship(s) positively and negatively?

_____

_____

_____

_____

_____

_____

_____

_____

_____

_____

What about being a woman do you love? Hate?

_____

_____

_____

_____

_____

_____

_____

_____

_____

What about being a woman do you feel you've lost touch with and want back in your life?

_____

_____

_____

_____

_____

_____

_____

_____

_____

_____

What changes do you intend to make about your femininity?

_____

_____

_____

_____

_____

_____

_____

_____

_____

_____

_____

What motivated you to read *The Proper Care and Feeding of Husbands*?

_____

_____

_____

_____

_____

_____

_____

_____

_____

_____

What feelings did you go through in reading the book?

_____

_____

_____

_____

_____

_____

_____

_____

_____

What less–than–positive wifely actions and attitudes did you recognize as yours?

_____

_____

_____

_____

_____

_____

_____

_____

_____

What more–than–positive wifely actions and attitudes did you recognize as yours?

_____

_____

_____

_____

_____

_____

_____

_____

_____

What was your husband's reaction to you reading the book?

_____

_____

_____

_____

_____

_____

_____

_____

How much do your less-than-wonderful actions and attitudes toward your husband have to do with your mother, sister, friends, media, vs. what you have always felt was right or comfortable?

_____

_____

_____

_____

_____

_____

_____

_____

_____

_____

What fantasies/expectations did you have about men and marriage before your marriage and how do you think that impacted your marital happiness?

_____

_____

_____

_____

_____

_____

_____

_____

_____

What did you imagine you'd always be *getting* from your husband and the marriage?

_____

_____

_____

_____

_____

_____

_____

_____

_____

_____

How did reality meet those expectations?

_____

_____

_____

_____

_____

_____

_____

_____

_____

What did you imagine you'd always be *giving* to your husband and your marriage?

_____

_____

_____

_____

_____

What do you enjoy about being a wife?

What do you not enjoy about being a wife?

What do you think would be the toughest thing about "you" coming home to you?

_____

What do you think is the loveliest thing about "you" coming home to you?

_____

How happy are you in your marriage?

_____

What do you believe your husband could do to make your marriage happier?

_____

_____

_____

_____

_____

_____

_____

_____

_____

What do you believe you could do to make your marriage happier?

_____

_____

_____

_____

_____

_____

_____

_____

_____

What stressors are there in your marriage that should be minimized or eliminated? How might you do that?

_____

_____

_____

_____

_____

_____

_____

_____

What do you plan to work on this week in terms of improving your attitude and/or your actions? (See next question)

_____

_____

_____

_____

_____

_____

_____

_____

_____

_____

_____

After one week from above, what changes have you noted in yourself and your husband?

_____

_____

_____

_____

_____

_____

_____

_____

_____

_____

_____

Your husband's turn:

This section will take courage and self-control to do. You will ask your husband for his input, and if you get "mad" or "hurt" over his answers, DO NOT LET HIM KNOW you are hurt, mad, or upset! If you want the truth, you've got to show you can handle the truth. Besides, showing him that you are open and willing to know his feelings, thoughts, and needs, is one of the most loving gifts a spouse can give. If you get all caught up in the "criticism," you'll miss the point that he feels safe coming to you. Where a man is safe, he will stay. Criticism is always hard to take, but it leads the way toward healing. Besides, you'll have your turn later!

Ask your husband to answer the following questions. Let him do it in private. And please, promise him you won't punish him for truthful answers that might be unflattering! Before you have your husband answer these questions, make a Xerox copy of these questions and write down the answers you imagine he'll give. Later you can compare them and discuss with him the similarities and the differences. (See Note below.)

What was your reaction to your wife's reading *TPCFH*?

What do you admire the most about women in general?

_____

_____

_____

_____

_____

_____

What do you most admire about your wife "as a woman"?

_____

_____

_____

_____

_____

_____

_____

_____

_____

_____

What do you think should be expected of you as a husband?

_____

_____

_____

_____

_____

_____

_____

_____

What do you think shouldn't be expected of you as a husband?

_____

_____

_____

_____
_____
_____
_____
_____
_____

What do you think should be expected of your wife?

_____
_____
_____
_____
_____
_____
_____
_____
_____
_____

What do you think shouldn't be expected of your wife?

_____
_____
_____
_____
_____
_____
_____
_____
_____

What aspects of your marriage hurt you the most?

_____
_____
_____

_____

_____

_____

_____

_____

_____

What aspects of your marriage are the most satisfying?

_____

_____

_____

_____

_____

_____

_____

_____

_____

_____

What is the difference between what you imagined marriage to be compared with what it is?

_____

_____

_____

_____

_____

_____

_____

_____

What do you imagine you are missing by being married?

_____

_____

_____

_____

_____

_____

_____

_____

_____

_____

_____

What do you realize/admit that you have stopped/started doing for your wife because of some hurt or disappointment in your marriage?

_____

_____

_____

_____

_____

_____

_____

_____

_____

_____

_____

_____

What do you long for from your wife?

_____

_____

_____

_____

_____

_____

_____

_____

_____

_____

_____

What specific changes would you like to see your wife make?

_____

_____

_____

_____

_____

_____

_____

_____

_____

_____

_____

_____

**What specific changes do you know you should make whether or
not your wife makes any?**

_____

_____

_____

_____

_____

_____

_____

_____

_____

Note: Please take the time right now to compare the answers your husband gave to the ones you imagined he'd give. It is important for you to be open to any differences so that communication between you and your husband stays open, honest, and constructive. Your role is to listen and ask questions, but not to defend, explain, excuse, argue, or attack. This is a critical exercise that, if done patiently and lovingly, will dramatically improve the feeling of safety, acceptance, and closeness between you and your husband.

This next section of the marital assessment takes place in person, with you, the wife, asking your husband the following questions. Again, do not react—just listen and learn! Anticipate that some of the answers might surprise or upset you. If you feel you can't deal with it, don't do it until you feel you can hear without judgment. Imagine how scared your husband is that you will become angry over his answers. Use that knowledge to temper your own reaction.

Ask your husband:

how he shows love

_____

_____

_____

_____

_____

_____

_____

_____

_____

how he defines "husband"

_____

_____

_____

_____

_____

_____

_____

_____

_____

how he defines "man/masculine"

_____

_____

_____

_____

_____

_____

_____

_____

_____

how you, his wife, make him feel about himself

_____

_____

_____

_____

_____

_____

_____

_____

_____

how he enjoys being a man, husband, and father

_____

_____

_____
_____
_____
_____
_____
_____
_____
_____

what he enjoys least about being a man, husband, and father

_____
_____
_____
_____
_____
_____
_____
_____
_____

how he feels about what he does for his family

_____
_____
_____
_____
_____
_____
_____
_____
_____

how he feels you respect him

_____

_____

_____

_____

_____

_____

_____

_____

_____

_____

how he knows when you're happy

_____

_____

_____

_____

_____

_____

_____

_____

_____

how he knows what you need/want

_____

_____

_____

_____

_____

_____

_____

_____

how he knows that you love him

_____
_____
_____
_____
_____
_____
_____
_____
_____
_____

how he knows that you need him

_____
_____
_____
_____
_____
_____
_____
_____
_____
_____

Without doubt, your conversation will expand into other areas. Please use the space below to reflect on this experience and its impact on you, your husband, and your relationship.

_____
_____
_____
_____
_____

_____

_____

_____

_____

_____

_____

_____

_____

_____

_____

_____

_____

_____

_____

In Part 3 you will deal with some prejudices and knee-jerk negative thinking you have about men and husbands, which may be getting in the way of you having the happy life you could have caring and feeding one of your very own!

PART THREE
Proper Respect:
Girls Rule—Boys Drool

Sensitivity Training and
Consciousness Raising

I admit it. I had a chuckle when writing the subtitle to this part of the companion book. I was in college in the '60s, when bras were burnt in anger against . . . well, everything was the sentiment of the times. "Consciousness raising" was the mantra of the feminist movement. We were to be perpetually aware of all the ways we were discriminated against and treated un-equally and unfairly (by gosh, even having a man open a door for us was considered a sexist-pig insult!) and warned about the determination of men to dominate and control us to nul-lify our value (beware of "barefoot and pregnant"!) through marriage and child-rearing.

I bought into it at the time. Why not? We women all thought we were establishing a new order of equality between the sexes and building a new power base for women to be unimpeded in their individual efforts to become doctors, astronauts, CEOs, or anything else they wanted. That still sounds right to me.

Several bad things came of that basically good idea. I don't believe that anyone with abilities and talents and the perseverance to develop them should be held back in contributing to the universe because of their gender. So far, so good. However, when things such as affirmative action and quotas came into being, equality and fairness went out the window, because ability became less important than the fact of genetics (XX vs. XY). Furthermore, women were made to feel more limited instead of less limited in their choices. If they wished to be wives and mothers (homemakers), they were disdained by their sisterhood, which condemned them as stupid, brainwashed, oppressed copouts. Motherhood and apple pie became bad. Women had to either shun love and family or "have it all"—and die an early death of unsatisfying stress and exhaustion or farm out children to secondary mothers (daycare and nannies) and just ignore their husbands; after all, any requests or needs of his were clearly intended to suffocate her as a woman!

Finally, the elevation of women was inexorably connected to a downgrading of men; not only were they the source of women's powerlessness and pain, the feminists still maintain, but they were not even necessary. Campuses across the country went as far as touting the superiority of intimate women-to-women relationships over that of a marriage.

I consider myself a feminist only in the original concept of equality of opportunity. I consider myself a recovered feminist in the context of the form of feminism that stole the movement. Devaluing the roles of wife and mother robbed women of an essential part of their spiritual, emotional, and physical destiny. I am thankful that at age thirty-five I had an epiphany and accepted that success needed a context to be perfected; the context was family.

Girls growing up in our present culture get few messages that make them feel special as women and respectful of their future mates. There is no support for feminine dignity or modesty. Thirteen-year-old girls are routinely performing oral sex on thirteen-year-old boys in classrooms (!) as a means of gaining (?) status; I think "good girls don't" was a better notion.

I get too many calls from women in their early twenties who are simply burned out with respect to love and marriage because of all the heartaches and heartbreaks they've experienced in too many "intimate" relationships while they sought equality through so-called free sex, which came at a devastating emotional price. They are hurt by the lack of form for "courtship," and the loss of the point of dating as a prelude to finding a mate. As they get older and even more cynical, their potential for marriage at all, much less a happy marriage, drops precipitously. They enter marriages guarded, suspicious, hypersensitive, and self-protective. Not good.

The brainwashing of women to feel hostile toward men begins in subtle and not-so-subtle ways, from the time they are little girls. The Associated Press (January 30, 2004) published a piece about a line of girls' clothes and accessories manufactured right here in the USA, which carried slogans like "Boys Are Stupid—Throw Rocks at Them," and "Boys Are Smelly—Throw Garbage Cans at Them," and "The Stupid Factory—Where Boys Are Made." Glenn Sacks, who hosts *His Side,* a weekly radio show aired in Los Angeles and Seattle that is sympathetic to fathers' rights, went on a campaign to have folks complain to the stores that sell these T-shirts. I backed him up.

In response to my joining the campaign, I received lots of faxes. One was from a woman who wears these T-shirts as an adult. She wrote,

> *"I love this shirt, it makes me laugh. It's just for FUN, if you can possibly remember the feeling. You're reading far too much into it. You've taken a T-shirt that was fun and harmless and turned it into something supposedly ugly and damaging. That's a shame."*

I am astounded by this woman's lack of sensitivity, the blindness to the pain these things can cause boys and men, not to mention the way they can tarnish the image of masculinity for girls at an early age.

Harmless . . . fun? Here's a response from an eight-year-old third-grader living in New Mexico.

> *"I am writing to you because of something that took place in my class. My class president is a fifth-grader who wore a T-shirt that said 'Boys Stink'—this really offended me, Dr. Laura. It made me feel really sad deep inside, because boys are not stupid and don't stink.*
>
> *"Without boys we wouldn't have husbands or children. I really think this company should be sued. I can't believe that this company has its own Web site that makes fun of boys and promotes violence toward them. On this Web site there are games that one plays to throw rocks at boys.*
>
> *"This is abuse for my gender. I will work for impeachment of my class president if she continues to wear this type of clothing."*

Breeding hostility between the sexes at the age of eight is harmless fun?

One adult female listener sent this e-mail to the manufacturer and distributor of these T-shirts:

> *"I just heard about your T-shirts on Dr. Laura. I am thirty-three years old and just getting married, hoping it's not too late to get pregnant. Know why? Negative opinions about men. I wasted years of my life thinking 'boys were stupid,' and that I didn't need them.*
>
> *"The subject matter of your shirts isn't good for anyone. I came to love men mostly on my own, thank God.*
>
> *"Men are smart, men are rational, men are brave! Men strive to improve the welfare of women and children. I'd wear a T-shirt like that!"*

Contrary to the prevalent feminist propaganda, one does not have to be antiboy to be profemale; yet that is exactly what has happened.

As one male listener shared:

"In one short generation, prevailing thought has gone from 'Father knows best,' all the way to 'Father is a bumbling imbecile, selfish, nasty, and violent to boot'!"

Another male listener complained that:

"I haven't yet read your book; however, I've been listening to your radio program, and it has created in me a fear for the future of my children and their understanding of their roles as men and women.

"I want the best for my children and want them to not be discriminated against in any form. It doesn't work that way. Our society seems to favor one to the detriment of the other. Or it feels it must punish one for the benefit of the other . . . It seems now there is a trend to create second-class citizens out of men and boys.

"Men, myself included, are on the defensive. We just don't know how to act or react these days, so we just say or do nothing, as that gets us in the least amount of trouble. Women can act as they want to, without a problem. Men can't—for fear of being labeled insensitive, chauvinist pig, or politically incorrect."

I recently went on a tear on my radio program concerning the infiltration of man-hating and heterophobic "entertainment" into our high schools and colleges in the form of a vulgar, mean play titled *The Vagina Monologues*. It unremittingly portrays men as the evil empire: rapists, aggressors, and predators. The production is offensive and horribly biased against men. In fifteen vignettes, women speak out as vaginas (so much for not reducing women to sex objects) discussing their experiences, including rape, lesbianism, and genital mutilation—as though American culture was known worldwide for its ex-

ploitation and abuse of women . . . oh please. Unbelievably, a se-
duction of a minor girl by an adult woman is presented as a
good thing, because she has learned she doesn't have to "rely on
a man."

I wonder why, though, in all the "feminist" statistics presented to drive their point home, they never mentioned (a) that
mothers are the number one murderers of small children, and (b)
that partner abuse figures in the homosexual and lesbian com-
munities match those of the heterosexual community.
Hmmmm.

As it turns out, according to FoxNews.com (January 27,
2004), one of the schools showcasing this trash turned down
the production of *West Side Story,* because it "promoted stereo-
types." I kid you not. I guess that to the feminists, ugly stereo-
types are not OK . . . unless they're about men.

I have received some criticisms and complaints that *TPCFH*
and my advice to women and wives is antifemale, because it en-
courages women to give up their thoughts and needs to please
some man. As I hope is clear by now, that's not true. But off-the-
mark hyperbole is the way that feminists strike back.

It is the intention of a "masculinist" movement in Canada
to promote a "male-friendly framework for understanding
social problems . . . The belief that equality between the sexes
requires the recognition and redress of prejudice and discrimi-
nation against men as well as women . . . A complementary, not
oppositional perspective to feminism."

The feminists came out of the woodwork to proclaim the
intentions of all "masculinists" as woman-hating creeps who
wish to "avoid child support, impoverish women, perpetuate a
patriarchal suprastructure by which women and children are
subjugated to property status."

Fortunately, groups like the Independent Women's Forum
(IWF) published an open memo to NOW (The National Organization of *I don't know what kind of* Women) that spoke of
"countless bright young women frustrated by rigid feminist
propaganda of male hatred . . ."

The only way this battle, the battle for equality of respect between the sexes, is going to be won is for the women to come out from under their defensive, hostile veils to find out the enemy is themselves.

Do you think I contend for one instant that some men aren't horrid creatures? No, of course not. But they are the exception, not the rule. As one male listener pointed out:

"There are, without question, some men out there that are deserving of the media and cultural bias that has plagued our country. There are, however, so many more men out there who are great fathers and great husbands."

Ironically, "liberated" women have created wussy Frankensteins out of men. More than a few times I have complained on my radio program that men seem to be emasculated and totally afraid of their women. Too many women in our society bully their men as though they were errant, annoying little boys rather than men worthy of respect and partners whom they need and want. The end result is that they behave badly, and then their women complain some more.

Men and women are different in almost every way possible, and, as one male listener observed:

". . . [women] have decided that since men are different than women that the men must be broken in some way, and it is their job to fix them."

The number-one means of "fixing" men is to transsexualize them—make them more like women. Men were perfected, the feminists proclaimed, by getting in touch with their "feminine side." Another male listener shared a quote from his favorite comedian: "My wife wanted me to get in touch with my feminine side. So I did. Turns out I'm a bitch." I love that.

Look, men and women are fundamentally *very* different. And different is not a judgment call, it is an observable fact. In fact, according to the Whitehead Institute in Cambridge, Massachussetts, ". . . men and women are more biologically different than was previously believed, right down to their genes . . . men and women differ genetically by 1 to 2 percent—as wide a gap as the one that separates women from female chimpanzees . . . the reality is that the genetic difference between males and females absolutely dwarfs all other differences in the human genome."

Instead of being threatened, cynical, or hateful about that difference, women and men should look at these differences as complementary and ultimately intimately satisfying. However, I can't believe how many times I've had to cajole some father into taking his rightful place of co-authority with his wife and *stand against* her allowing their daughter to date much older boys or wear inappropriate Britney Spears, slut-style clothing; or *stand with* his son's desire to take martial arts or train with firearms. The men are afraid of their wives' punishment (anger, yelling, pouting, more no-sex) if they speak up, and have collapsed into a heap of castrated protoplasm.

Civilization requires strong men. Family security requires strong men. Real women love strong men. Real women are not intimidated nor consider themselves oppressed by strong men. A real women sees a strong man as a counterpart and a completion.

When the feminist-controlled, politically correct culture is not pointing the damning finger at men for being the sole problem in any woman's life, it is laughing in disrespect at jokes demeaning men as husbands and fathers.

Over the years I've received hundreds of Internet lists of jokes about men. Here's but one:

> *Men are like . . . Placemats. They only show up when there's food on the table.*

> *Men are like . . . Mascara. They usually run at the first sign of emotion.*

> *Men are like . . . Bike helmets. Handy in an emergency, but otherwise they just look silly.*

Men are like . . . Government bonds.
They take so long to mature.

Men are like . . . Lava lamps. Fun to look at
but not all that bright.

Men are like . . . Bank accounts. Without a lot of money they
don't generate much interest.

Men are like . . . High heels. They're easy to walk on
once you get the hang of it.

This letter was sent by a woman who received this "joke" in her e-mail. She wrote, "Do you know of anything cleverly written that is positive about men that I can use to rebut this so-called humor?" I didn't have a resource to give her.

It is clear that women are immersed in an antimale climate, be it media, their mothers, girlfriends, magazines, or schools. This antimale attitude negatively impacts women's respect, acceptance, appreciation, and sensitivity toward the men in their lives. How can a woman "become one" with an entity that is disdained? How can a woman "become one" with a man she is told to suspect or be defensive about? How can a woman "become one" with a man, when she is lead to believe that when she is loving, giving, and nurturing to her man, she has lost her self? How can a woman "become one" with a man when she has been told that she is the center of her universe; that mothering, or homemaking, and loving her husband are beneath a woman?

How, indeed.

Your turn:

This exercise will help you to recognize, evaluate, and become more aware and sensitive to the antimale bias you probably experience on a daily basis. It is likely that you aren't even aware of how this input influences your attitudes and reactions to your husband. Please observe and record any instances of gratuitous printed, viewed, or spoken insensitivity, hostility, negative stereotyping, disdainful gossiping, and down-right meanness toward men that you encounter daily for at least one week.

TV:

_____

_____

_____

_____

_____

_____

_____

_____

_____

Magazines and Newspapers:

_____

_____

_____

_____

_____

_____

_____

_____

Your Friends:

_____

_____

_____

_____

_____
_____
_____
_____
_____

Radio:

_____
_____
_____
_____
_____
_____
_____
_____
_____

The Internet:

_____
_____
_____
_____
_____
_____
_____
_____

Your Adult Female Relatives:

_____
_____
_____

_____
_____
_____
_____
_____
_____
_____
_____

Your Children:

_____
_____
_____
_____
_____
_____
_____
_____
_____
_____

Movies, Books, Plays, Music:

_____
_____
_____
_____
_____
_____
_____
_____
_____
_____

Please record any instances in which you found yourself generalizing negatives about men in general or your husband in particular. Explore what was gained (acceptance, relief of frustrations, etc.).

_____

_____

_____

_____

_____

_____

_____

_____

_____

Please consult with the men in your life (father, husband, brothers, sons) about their experiences with antimale prejudices.

_____

_____

_____

_____

_____

_____

_____

_____

_____

What do you believe you learned about femininity and masculinity from your mother and father?

_____

_____

_____

_____

_____

_____

_____

_____

_____

_____

_____

Please think about and write down your memories of learning about what boys and men were about and the feelings you've had about them throughout the stages of your life.

_____

_____

_____

_____

_____

_____

_____

_____

_____

What thoughts do you have concerning your own participation in the societal disdain and negativity toward masculinity?

_____

_____

_____

_____

_____

_____

_____

_____

List and describe the negative attitudes and images about men that you believe you may have "bought into."

_____
_____
_____
_____
_____
_____
_____
_____
_____

Describe those negative attitudes about men/masculinity which you believe you may have incorporated into your own way of looking at men and relationships.

_____
_____
_____
_____
_____
_____
_____
_____
_____
_____

Please write about your positive notions of men and masculinity—those qualities you seek out and admire in a man; what are they and where did you get those positive notions?

_____
_____
_____
_____

_____

_____

_____

_____

_____

Please write about the qualities of the men (husbands, brothers, fathers, uncles, grandfathers, in-laws) and boys (sons, nephews) in your life and how you see, judge, and treat them within the context of the antimale generalities you have already described.

_____

_____

_____

_____

_____

_____

_____

_____

What do you think you might do to counteract the numerous sources of negativity toward men/masculinity?

_____

_____

_____

_____

_____

_____

_____

_____

Other thoughts and questions?

PART FOUR

Proper Understanding: The Guys' Turn!

What the Heck Are Men Thinking, Needing, and Wanting?

Even with a span of thirty years on radio, a decade of private practice, and fifty-seven years of life, not until I did the preparation for, and writing of, this book, did I realize that husbands as a group were largely unhappy.

The typical complaints that men have about women have been largely discounted—by women—as just "the way it is": Women are mercurial in their moods what with menstrual cycles, pregnancies, and moon spots (it's a woman's prerogative); critical (but it's for your own good, guys, we're just trying to straighten you out!); emotionally reactive (hey, you do X and you don't expect a reaction?); punitive when crossed (I'm not in the mood, honey); circuitous in their communication (no means maybe, or actually a yes, but we want you to guess which); insistent that feelings always trump reason (there is no "right answer"—and if there were, it would be open to change at any time); and basically unpredictable in all of the above.

Be honest. What man has ever felt that he understood women? That breeds a certain amount of helplessness, which breeds a certain amount of hopelessness, which breeds a certain amount of unhappiness, and unhappy men eventually give up trying to please or relate to their women.

But what do women understand about their men? I believe men try really hard to "get" us. I believe women don't try very hard to "get" men. In fact, I believe that we women think it isn't very important to try to "get" men. And we become very defensive when the suggestion is made that we ought to understand our men better. As I have pointed out early in this book, women have been groomed always to make sure that they get what they want from their men, and believe they are entitled to all that regardless of how satisfied the men are in the relationship. When criticized by our men, we yell, or cry, or both . . . and the discussion ends.

Ever hear the old saying, "Happier cows give more milk"? Well, works for bulls too—except for the milk part.

The following bit of humor, obviously written by a man, is really more of a husband's lament. While this is worth many chuckles, there is much that women ought to think about.

A female listener, "hoping to improve [herself] by reading *The Proper Care and Feeding of Husbands,* forwarded the following "joke" that has been circulating on the Internet.

Please note . . . these are all numbered "1" on purpose:
1. *Learn to work the toilet seat. You're a big girl. If it's up, put it down. We need it up, you need it down. You don't hear us complaining about you leaving it down!*
1. *Sunday=Sports. It's like the full moon or the changing of the tides. Let it be.*
1. *Shopping is NOT a sport. And no, we are never going to think of it that way.*
1. *Crying is blackmail.*
1. *Ask for what you want. Let us be clear on this one:*

Subtle hints do not work! Strong hints do not work! Obvious hints do not work! Just say it!

1. *Yes or No are perfectly acceptable answers to almost every question.*
1. *Come to us with a problem only if you want help solving it. That's what we do. Sympathy is what your girlfriends are for.*
1. *A headache that lasts for 17 months is a problem. See a doctor.*
1. *Anything we said 6 months ago is inadmissible in an argument. In fact, all comments become null and void after 7 days.*
1. *If you won't dress like the Victoria's Secret girls, don't expect us to act like soap opera guys.*
1. *If you think you're fat, you probably are—don't ask us.*
1. *If something we said can be interpreted two ways, and one of the ways makes you sad or angry, we meant the other one.*
1. *You can either ask us to do something or tell us how you want it done. Not both. If you already know best how to do it, just do it yourself.*
1. *Whenever possible, please say whatever you have to say during commercials.*
1. *ALL men see in only 16 colors, like Windows default settings. Peach, for example, is a fruit, not a color. Pumpkin is also a fruit. We have no idea what mauve is.*
1. *If it itches, it will be scratched.*
1. *If we ask what is wrong and you say "nothing," we will act like nothing's wrong. We know you are lying, but it is just not worth the hassle.*
1. *If you ask a question you don't really want us to answer, expect an answer you don't want to hear.*
1. *When we go somewhere, absolutely anything you wear is fine . . . really.*
1. *Don't ask us what we're thinking about unless you are prepared to discuss such topics as baseball, the shotgun information, or monster trucks.*

1. *You have enough clothes.*
1. *You have too many shoes.*
1. *I am in shape; round is a shape.*
1. *Thank you for reading this. Yes, I know I have to sleep on the couch tonight, but did you know men really don't mind that? It's like camping.*

Another Internet "joke" was sent to me by a woman who lost her husband to cancer. She wrote that she thinks they had a pretty good marriage, but

"... *if I had only had* The Proper Care *before his death, we could have had a wonderful marriage, if I had only known how to do it. They send us to college so we can gain the knowledge to have a great profession, but somewhere we missed finding the knowledge on how to have a great marriage and home life. I just hope and pray that someday I get an opportunity to use all this newfound knowledge and make a great marriage.*

"*One of my coworkers sent me this:*

How to impress a woman: *wine her; dine her; call her; hug her; support her; hold her; surprise her; compliment her; smile at her; listen to her; laugh with her; cry with her; romance her; encourage her; believe in her; pray with her; pray for her; cuddle with her; shop with her; give her jewelry; buy her flowers; hold her hand; write love letters to her; go to the end of the Earth and back again for her.*

How to impress a man: *show up naked, bring chicken wings and beer ... don't block the TV.*"

See? I said men were simple!

Before we go on with the ten questions I asked my male listeners about how their needs and feelings are being met in their marriages, I think it's important that you wives go back over these "jokes" and think about how much we women take for granted in our everyday lives with our men.

Your turn:

For the most part, do you think these all "# 1" comments are fair or not? If so, why so—if not, why not? Do Part 2 of this question one week later.

_____

_____

_____

_____

_____

_____

_____

_____

_____

Part 2: In what way(s) have you changed your position(s) on the above question one week later . . . having been more attentive to the male-female interactions in your home (and others')?

_____

_____

_____

_____

_____

_____

_____

_____

In reviewing the substance of the "jokes," what issues did you recognize influencing your own attitudes and behaviors with your husband (boyfriend, fiancé)?

_____

_____

_____

_____

_____

_____

_____

_____

_____

Pick three issues or points you know you ought to work on. Please list them below and record your progress over one week's time. Then, review a month later.

1.

_____

_____

_____

_____

_____

2.

_____

_____

_____

_____

_____

3.

_____

_____

_____

_____

_____

One month later:

1.

_____

_____

_____

_____

_____

2.

_____

_____

_____

_____

3.

_____

_____

_____

_____

To help clarify for wives what their men really want, I put ten questions on my Web site and asked men who had read part or all of *The Proper Care and Feeding of Husbands* to answer. Generally, when it comes to dealing with relationship issues, men don't volunteer easily, because they believe (a) no one is *really* listening, (b) they don't have the power to change much, (c) they are outgunned by their verbally superior and angry (defensive) wives, (d) they'll probably be indicted as wrong anyway, so why bother, and (e) they've learned to sublimate their emotions in work, sports, hobbies, children, television, or alcohol. These sentiments often keep them from seeking marital therapy.

Fortunately, the number of responses was overwhelming! I am grateful that so many men felt safe enough to express their deepest feelings about their wives, love, and marriage. It is interesting and important to note that in the hundreds of responses there weren't hundreds of *different* responses. What was important to each man seemed to be important to almost all the men. Therefore, I will summarize the more typical answers after each question. We women need to take these responses to heart.

Question 1: *What part(s) of the book were "right on" for your marriage?*

I should note that by the time all the answers were "tallied," each part of the book was found to be applicable in some way to some men. Below are "typical" responses:

1. "The explanation about how the feminist movement has negatively impacted our generation and that of our daughters."

2. "My wife's life is filled with things that must be done. If listed in priority, my needs would be somewhere after 'rearrange the sock drawer.' I went from #1 to #101 in twenty-five years."

3. "The part about a man doing anything for his wife is right on. I took a job specifically so my wife would stay home with our kids. I did this even though I loved my original job and simply hated my new, higher-paying job. I did it for her."

4. "The unspoken message that men are not a legitimate concern of women. They can take care of themselves, and that women are the oppressed and the men the oppressors. . . . Women are so self-centered and thinking that the whole world revolves around them. Some women have the attitude that they are entitled to everything: a career, a perfect husband, kids, free time, material things, a nice home, servants, and that everyone

should drop their own lives and make that all happen for them."

5. "That it is not 'shallow' to want sex; to want to be thought a hero; to want to be admired; to want to be appreciated. That it's not 'better' to be female. That we like when they initiate sex sometimes; shows us they find us appealing."

6. "I have studied many relationship books and always felt the onus was on the men to do whatever it takes to appease their wives. I had resigned myself to the idea that this is as good as it gets."

7. "The move from the loving wife (and boy, was she loving!) to the dutiful mother. She has not, in nineteen years, made the switch back."

8. "The lack of proper understandable communication. Lack of praise and appreciation. Sex as weapon or tool. Her not understanding how men behave and react to statements."

9. "Their 'big gun' is, 'You hurt my feelings.'"

10. "I love my wife very much, but after working a full day and coming home and helping with dinner, homework, and putting the kids to bed, I was still getting 'fussed at' for not doing the laundry right, not dusting the right way, and hearing that 'No one is helping around the house and she can't do it all herself.'"

11. "I have mentioned to my wife before that I feel like I'm just a paycheck and slave to her. It is wearing to go through life and feel that masculinity is considered worthless to the majority of women. Ignore us and we will feel rejected and lost and become distant and moody. Just pay attention to us, let us know you care. Save a little of yourself to share with your husband. Do not give 100 percent of yourself to the rest of the world and have nothing left for him."

12. "My wife takes a very aggressive and supercritical approach to me, and is also so delicate herself that any response from me is unacceptable, and I am gross, uncaring, and insensitive. If I express to my wife that something makes me uncomfortable, I was controlling. If I told her not to talk to me in a certain manner, I was controlling. However, if she leveraged her disapproving looks and condescending words to cut me down and influence my behavior, speech, and principles, she was in no way controlling me."

13. "I have done a lot of work on myself as a human, man, husband, but no matter how much work I do I can never outrun the monster of the past. My wife still, when she is mad or doesn't want to take blame for something she has done wrong, throws that back in my face in defense."

14. "A man is so simple to understand. Just quit fighting us and seeing us as the enemy. I need routine, I need my dignity, I need my family; and for this, my sons get a dad for life and my wife gets a man who would die for her. It is so simple."

15. "I think most women do not know how to communicate with men. Usually we are talked to as if we were a girlfriend. Men in general are much more specific in communication. Women also think we are not easily hurt verbally. With a woman a man loves, a look, a stare, something said 'under the breath' can stick a man emotionally worse than a knife."

Your turn:

Please read through this list to see if any of these laments could be describing your husband's perspective. Try to be fair, nondefensive, and open. Remember, the more you know and understand about your man's "simple needs," the more you can use your power to make your life happier. Admitting that one has been blind, insensitive, or stubborn, while not pleasant, is the key to the treasure chest of peace and joy in home and your life.

_____

_____

_____

_____

_____

_____

_____

_____

_____

_____

_____

_____

_____

_____

_____

_____

_____

_____

Question 2: *What do you think most women don't get about men/masculinity?*

1. "They desire for a man to be masculine (strong) but want to control him (weak). What most women don't get is that men need to be masculine. Their attempts to control a man only serves to either emasculate him or cause 'irreconcilable differences.'

   "Men have so few areas where they are allowed to be the sole decision maker that when a need to direct the situation arises it is mistakenly viewed as controlling."

2. "To serve is our God-given purpose. Women don't get that men want to do things for their wives that will make them happy. However, when wives aren't ever happy, men don't want to do anything for them. The attitude of gratitude toward a man is now an attitude of entitlement: you owe me!"

3. "The best way to increase golf memberships or to sell fishing boats is to have wives withhold sex. Whether a man has his own business or a job, he realizes that he must work before he gets paid. As long as they are reassured that payment will be made when the work is done, he does his best with a good attitude. When payment isn't made, it doesn't take long for resentment to grow and to think he might as well go golfing."

4. "Women don't understand that lovemaking IS a man's way of saying, 'I love you.' Lovemaking is such an important part of a man's life. Having a guy 'beg' for lovemaking, rejecting him, or making it quick to get it out of the way leads to relationship problems (masturbation, porn, fantasies about other women, prostitutes, workaholism, taking it out on the kids, and so forth)."

5. "Women have NOT cornered the market on feelings. Men feel and become hurt, just like women do. I'm a man and I have dreams. I have fantasies about romance and love. I feel disappointments, just like women do. Also, most women have no clue how much work and stress men face every day in supporting a family. That is a lot of responsibility."

6. "We like to get dirty, smell bad, and be rough around the edges from time to time."

7. "Women don't get that men need positive strokes, just like they do. I frequently compliment and thank my wife if she irons my shirts (rarely, for sure), any time it's obvious that she put any effort at all into dinner, helping the boys with school work, etc. The reverse is seldom true."

8. "I believe our purpose is like what you see on police cars in some towns, 'To Protect and Serve.' Society has feminized the picture of the traditional male to fit the unisex, passive, and nonconfrontational expectations. We need to feel appreciated as protectors, providers, lovers, and conquerors."

9. "I know she needed to talk, but couldn't we at least show some happiness in seeing each other first, and maybe a hug and a kiss? I loved to hug and embrace, and, while we were dating, she did, too, but after we were married, her enjoyment of it soon tapered off."

10. "Lack of understanding male pressures in making a living and supporting family."

11. "Women don't seem to get that men simply need to be respected and their woman's behavior provides it. We want to be first in our woman's life. They don't seem to get that men seek a safe preserve from the battles they fight outside the home; the safe preserve is provided by their woman. If men get these things, they will fight to the death for their woman and children."

12. "If you're a good, faithful, strong man, you want to be fed, loved, and admired for something. It gives the confidence to conquer. They do not understand that we love them, not some picture of beauty but them. We have made a sacrifice to be faithful to one woman and would fight off every bear to protect them if they would just let us. They don't understand that wanting to change us robs us of our fundamental manhood and makes us something they don't really want."

Your turn:

Please review these twelve points. Note which is a surprise to you or a reminder for you. Think about how often you measure his actions by a feminine standard of emotional reaction or behavior. Think also about how often you try to change him rather than understand him and accept him on his own merits. Compare/contrast masculine/feminine traits without criticism—just by description. Come back to this one month later to reassess what has changed in your thinking and reacting to your man based on your knowledge and acceptance of "masculinity" traits.

One month later:

Question 3: *What does being a "man" mean to you?*

1. "That I take active responsibility for myself and others around me. That doesn't mean that I control others, but it means that I must see to others' needs and hold them accountable for their actions as it is appropriate to do so."

2. "Taking care of your family, having complete fidelity to your wife, and living up to the ideals that you espouse."

3. "We are the engines to getting things done and the defenders of virtue. We are here to protect and serve and it is a privilege."

4. "Seeking adventure; being courageous; being a hero; taking care of family; loving God."

5. "Being a man is being the pillar of strength, the composed, unemotional one. Level-headed and driven by reason, not emotion."

6. "Taking on and performing your responsibilities no matter what the rewards are or are not. Having integrity and being honest."

7. "It means being an honest, hardworking husband and father, a good provider and protector, and also to be a leader in times of emergency and crisis and to be mindful of the many needs of my wife and children—who are my life. Everything I do, I do for them."

8. "Being a parent to your kids and teaching them about life, religion, relationships, proper behavior, and problem-solving."

9. "Being strong and having courage. Placing my own desires after those of my family. Providing for my family without whining or complaining. Looking at life's issues with objective rather than subjective viewpoint and providing leadership based on that viewpoint."

10. "It means to constructively express every male tendency that is hard-wired into my brain. That doesn't mean farting, scratching, and watching porn. It means leading my family, growing my business, screaming and hollering at the game on TV, protecting my children, and [regularly] making love to my wife. It also means doing everything I can to raise my sons to be proud of who they are and to help them be a model of the constructive male stereotype."

11. "A man does what he knows is right, regardless of how he feels. A man will do the right thing even if it causes him pain. A man gets out of bed every morning and works to support his family, whether he has a fulfilling job or not. A man is gentle and kind to his wife and children. A man should never be 'me first.'"

12. "Being a man means providing physical and financial security to my woman and children. It means being rock-stable, confident, and strong. It means being courageous, virtuous, and noble. It means being inspirational and fully devoted and committed to my wife and children. It means being an example of strong character and integrity to my children."

Your turn:

It seems really clear that men believe that their role is to protect and serve. I don't believe that is a societal invention—I believe it is built into the DNA. Please consider how men see their place in the world as serving their families first, and think about how cultural pressures have thwarted the expression of that need and devalued it in the eyes of men and women.

Ask your husband how he gets to express "being a man." Remember, just listen—don't criticize or challenge.

_____

_____

_____

_____

_____

_____

_____

_____

_____

_____

_____

_____

_____

_____

_____

_____

_____

_____

Question 4: *What is the most hurtful thing your wife can say or do to you?*

1. "Disrespect. Trashing me to her friends, our children."

2. "Telling me what I missed when I take an hour to clean something."

3. " 'That's all you think about . . . let's get it over with quickly!' "

4. " 'If you don't ___, then I'm leaving.' "

5. "She makes me feel insignificant. I have expressed that I am lonely, unhappy, depressed, and need to talk to her about our relationship. Her response? 'I don't have time right now.' She NEVER has time."

6. "Withhold her affection from me, whether it is physical or emotional. I need her. She is the one person who possesses my heart."

7. "Placing other things ahead of me—especially our children or her relatives. Seeing her making sacrifices and finding time to do for others, but not having time or willingness to sacrifice to do the things I ask."

8. "Ignore me. If she rejects me, it is better than just ignoring me."

9. "Call me, my words, or my values stupid. Say or imply that I am not needed. Call me needy when I ask for anything in the relationship. Make me feel like whatever I do, it's never enough."

10. "Always correcting me because I don't say what she thinks I should have said. Accusing me of being mean when I don't want to do what she wants."

11. "The most painful thing my wife can do is express disapproval for the way I have done something, or act disappointed when an act of kindness or a gift isn't quite what she wanted."

12. "The most hurtful thing she does to me is not acknowledging her love for me and things I do for her out of love and caring."

13. "She's never satisfied. We have the big house, cars, etc., but I never got the feeling of 'Hello, this is my husband, and he is enough!'"

Your turn:

Please take the time to review the answers above. What are the core issues being expressed? Try to imagine your marriage from his point of view. Write down your actions you believe your husband is likely to be thinking about. Come up with some ways to repair the situation.

_____

_____

_____

_____

_____

_____

_____

_____

_____

_____

Question 5: *What is the most wonderful thing your wife can say or do?*

1. "Initiate a romantic encounter. Be as excited about physical intimacy as I am."

2. "Say 'thank you' or 'I love you' without my coaxing it out of her or without me saying it first."

3. "Just be happy."

4. " 'I appreciate you; you're my hero; do you want (sex)?'"

5. "That she would marry me all over again."

6. "Pull up a lawn chair while I am working and read a book and just watch and talk a little and admire the man she is with."

7. "It's really wonderful when she dresses up, does her hair and makeup, and puts on perfume just for me!"

8. "Be a 'girl' and use her charms on me."

9. "Say 'I'm sorry' when she's wrong."

10. "It's all in the little things that stroke my ego and make me feel like 'the man.'"

11. "Greet me, when I come home, with a hug and a kiss and let me know that she is glad to have me around."

12. "The most wonderful thing she could do for me would
be to truthfully let me know I make her happy, and she
appreciates what I do (not superficially, but on a real
level), and finally, that she would like to stay with me
even after we leave these bodies."

13. "Ask me about something and not interrupt when I try
to answer."

14. "When she says, 'What would you like for your birthday
or Christmas?' I say, 'You—naked.' That must be really
hard because I usually end up with a shirt."

15. "When she tells me she loves me, and holds me."

16. "Be satisfied with who and what I am."

Your turn:

If you ever wondered what in the world he needs to be happy, I believe this list
makes it clear—and makes it clear how simple it is to please your man. The A's
have it again: appreciation, attention, affection, approval. Start noting the times
you do any of these A's—and pay attention to the immediate and longer-term
responses.

Question 6: *What is the toughest part of being a man?*

1. "Doing a lot of work without much recognition for my efforts."

2. "It's being in a relationship where there's little or no appreciation, most everything is a problem, and I'm not enough."

3. "Having so many responsibilities—so much to live up to—without showing weaknesses. Carrying on when you are tired, discouraged, or sick."

4. "Trying to be all things to all people. Being expected to work all day to earn a living for the family, then come home and be expected to help all night around the house, and being there for the kids to do homework, say prayers, and help with projects. No one seems to understand that every now and then we need a little time to ourselves without being made to feel that we are just wasting time when we could be doing something more productive."

5. "Mind-reading. When my wife is obviously upset about something or me, and I question her about it, there are usually three answers: 'Nothing,' or 'If you don't know then I'm not going to tell you,' or 'I don't know.'"

6. "Our wives complain about our male tendencies and yet deep down they really do want a protector and a provider. Yet they are so torn by angry feminists, bad press, poor guidance, and screwed-up friends, that they are almost schizophrenic in their attempts to create a husband that is strong yet sensitive, individualistic yet conforming, passive yet warlike, successful but only to the extent it doesn't inconvenience their needs. Society has so totally screwed up the image of what is male that it is no surprise there are so many confused guys out there."

7. "Having to not show your true feelings when your wife hurts you. Having to stay strong when you feel like breaking down and crying from the hurt."

8. "Being confused about feelings and emotions. Men don't talk about feelings and emotions the same way as women. I believe that you can set a task in front of a man and he'll figure out a way to get the job done. But when it comes to communicating feelings and emotions clearly, or understanding your partner's feelings and emotions, it's tougher than the toughest job. I would rather get into a boxing ring with a prizefighter than experience a difficult, emotional moment with my wife. I guess you could say it scares me because I don't know what to do."

9. "Being automatically perceived as an insensitive, selfish moron."

10. "You are pretty much alone. There isn't much emotional support for men."

11. "Knowing that ultimately you are totally responsible for everything. Failure is harder on a man because there are no excuses! My experience in family law has impressed on me that there has NEVER been a woman that considered herself even 25 percent at fault for a failed marriage, even if her adultery ended the marriage."

Your turn:

Please review these answers and think about how often those in your life (friends, family, etc.) ever show compassion for men. It is easy to ignore the nonsqueaky wheel; what might you be missing about what your husband deals with by virtue of his being male? How do you think you've added to/subtracted from his "burdens?"

A reminder: it is too easy to slip into the "I have problems, too!" mode. Try to not go there. Try to stay in the mode of understanding him. Don't compete, don't defend yourself, don't criticize, and don't argue. Just be there for him in your mind and heart. The payback will be a multitude of blessings.

_____

_____

_____

_____

_____

_____

_____

_____

_____

_____

_____

_____

_____

_____

_____

Question 7: *If your wife has read the book, what changes has she instituted?*

1. "I immediately noticed a change, as her response to me softened."

2. "She is only on chapter 3, but so far, so good! In our new metaphor, she has already made two sandwiches for me." *(Author's note:* In *The Proper Care and Feeding of Husbands* introduction, there was a letter from "John," which talked about men being simple in their needs. "If we're not horny, then make us a sandwich," was his comment.)

3. "Less judgmental. More apt to lay decision in my hands without having to second-guess my motivation. What you have established, Dr. Laura, is that marriage is similar to a religion. If you believe in God, you surrender conundrums to Him, with a restful outlook on life."

4. "First, she has worked to appreciate the things that I do around the house and with our daughter to ease her burden. She tended, especially after a stressful day, to be difficult to please. Second, she didn't realize that I needed to feel that she cared about the state of my

'castle.' She now has invested herself in our home, and is working to make it a haven after a long day at work."

5. "Amazing changes in one week! She has initiated sex two times and there haven't been complaints or arguments!"

6. "She has been more loving and complimentary—not that she was bad before. I am married to an incredible woman."

7. "We cried and prayed together. She told me she was sorry for taking me for granted and paying attention to everything else but me. It was wonderful. I am grateful."

8. "It has served to make my wife more sensitive to my need for us to find time to be intimate."

Your turn:
Please contemplate these questions:

1. Do you find yourself uncomfortable making changes in your behavior toward him? What do you think contributes to that discomfort and what can you do to get past it?

_____

_____

_____

_____

_____

_____

_____

_____

_____

2. What is the scariest thing about being more attentive and affectionate with him?

_____

_____

3. What support or negativity are you getting from your close women friends about the changes you are making in your marriage/relationship?

4. What do you believe is/are the core reason(s) that some women are offended by, hostile to, or rejecting of reading *The Proper Care and Feeding of Husbands?*

5. As a wife yourself, what would be your best counterargument to #4?

_____

_____

_____

_____

_____

_____

_____

_____

_____

6. How will having read *The Proper Care and Feeding of Husbands* and this workbook affect what you teach your daughter about marriage and men?

_____

_____

_____

_____

_____

_____

_____

_____

_____

Question 8: *What changes have you made in response to Question # 7?*

1. "I always appreciate it when my wife fixes anything, even if it's just a hot dog. Now that she buys some of the foods I like, I tell her I noticed and appreciated that, too."

2. "I am much more mindful that she is trying hard to be nice and to please me. It makes me want her all the

more and to please her. I now want to spend my whole life with just her."

3. "I don't feel like I am always on the defensive when I get home, and I don't dread opening the door when I'm late. I still try to do as much as I can when I get home, but our night is much more pleasant, and we have more quiet time. I also try harder to leave work on time."

4. "I am constantly trying to figure out how I can help my wife with her life—so that her life will be less complicated, less stressful."

5. "I have attempted to be more sensitive to her priorities when helping around the house. I am also working to read her moods better and bring up issues when she is less stressed."

6. "How can I be a grouchy jerk when she is treating me with so much love? I am a lot less self-centered."

7. "I believe I am more conversant with her, expressing my answers to her comments and questions more completely, carefully, and thoughtfully. I probably feel a little safer to speak. I believe she likes this."

8. "I don't hide in my basement office playing computer games to avoid her routine coldness anymore. It's like we're girlfriend and boyfriend again. I don't have to be nagged to be with her. I now look forward to it."

Your turn:

What are the subtle and blatant changes you have noticed in your husband since you started reading the book?

_____

_____

_____

_____

_____

What are some of the positive things you've started to notice and appreciate about your husband?

In what way does it actually surprise you that you've been successful in transforming your husband's demeanor and behaviors without nagging?

This would be a good time to sit with a group of your friends and talk about your fathers and mothers and the issue of who really was in emotional control. Would you say that "on the average" men have to be "careful" around their women, because of the unpredictability of their emotional response and the fear of "crossing them?"

_____

_____

_____

_____

_____

_____

_____

_____

_____

_____

_____

Would you say that women have designed lives which are so stressful that they can't "stop and smell the roses" in their own marriages? Why? And how can that be changed?

_____

_____

_____

_____

_____

_____

_____

_____

_____

_____

_____

_____

Question 9: *What are the benefits/negatives of marriage for a man?*

1. "There are negatives? Even with our sex challenges, it's better than outright loneliness. My wife is a dear and the kids are a great blessing from God."

2. "The benefits are the satisfaction of taking care of your wife and family. The negatives are that I don't always get the recognition that I want and that we only have sex about four times a year."

3. "The benefit would be a purpose in life. The negative would be that being a man in my house is a forsaken role, resented and despised for no logical reason other than that I am a man. My wife learned from her mother that men were a necessary evil. My role is hell."

4. "I have been blessed with my best friend and four great kids who are healthy, happy, and extremely talented—which comes from their mother. Marriage provides direction and purpose to my life and a sense of accomplishment. I can't think of any concrete negatives, and if I did, I wouldn't dwell on them, since changing my life is not an option."

5. "Benefit: FAMILY. I adore my family! Negative: not being able to do things without family, like fishing."

6. "Benefits are many! I love being married. I feel I'm healthier for it. I have a loving wife to care for me and to watch over my well-being. She is the one person in the world who cares for me. The negatives to marriage are that there is little opportunity to chase after adventures. I'd love to sail yachts in competition or collect sports cars. Being married means that my family duties and responsibilities come first."

7. "Benefit: being in a loving relationship with your wife and family. Being respected, looked up to. Having a long-term GREAT sex life. Being a parent: teaching, coaching,

helping with homework, seeing/being involved in their growth. Going to church as a family, sitting in a pew in front of God and worshiping together. Having a mate to do things with. Negative: marrying the wrong person and then most of the above doesn't happen."

8. "You have someone to curl up with on the couch or keep you warm at night. Sex on demand—supposedly. Sharing the joy of building together—starting without much of anything and working to having a stable and prosperous household. Negative: PMS."

9. "Actually, I like marriage. I just don't like being married to the woman I'm married to. Marriage is a way to share the burden of everyday living and share of yourself. Unfortunately, that doesn't happen in our marriage. If my wife shares with anyone, it's her mother. She treats her mother like a goddess and my son and me like bums. I wouldn't treat a dog the way my wife treats me."

10. "The benefits are I have a wife and kids that I love and who love me in return. I would do anything for my family. The negatives are I don't seem to have any free time to go out and relax or just sit down at home without feeling that I am expected to do something for someone else."

11. "The benefits would be having someone to love, to live for, to know that at least you made one person's life happier; and to have a friend who would be with you no matter what. The negatives are when you get tied up in so many small negatives and forget the love, which makes everything else just minor details."

12. "The benefits of a positive marriage are the rewards of marrying a woman who will grow with you. A woman who will allow you to serve as her champion, yet, at the same time, through her efforts, will become your champion. A good marriage is like finding a best friend of the opposite sex whose relationship with you is ad-

vanced by the presence of children, and the sheer, un-complicated, unending joy of sex. There is no negative to a good marriage."

13. "If a marriage is good, there really are no negatives to marriage for a man. The benefits are many: friendship, affection, someone to share everything with, improved health, better diet, warmer nights, someone who notices if your tie doesn't match. On the other hand, there are many negatives to a marriage if it is poor. A man has more expendable cash when single. A man in a poor marriage is constantly being run down; he feels that he can never be good enough. A married man has no security; she can leave him anytime the moon spots are wrong, and take the kids, most of his assets, and a significant portion of his income for much of his remaining life."

14. "All marriage is a benefit to real men. For a man, all marriage is about the taming of the strong, masculine inclinations that can either be constructive, if encouraged by an insightful woman, or destructive if left untamed. A boy with normal, positive, masculine traits becomes a man when he shares his life with a woman who provides life's purpose within the family. The man may be responsible for so much of the vitality that surrounds a family; yet it is the woman who softens this vitality toward the betterment of the family and the children within the family."

Your turn:
What do you see as the common threads of these answers?

Consider #14. Explore the concept of woman taming man. How important have you believed women were in shaping a man's behavior?

_____

_____

_____

_____

_____

_____

_____

_____

Consider how you've "tamed" your husband.

_____

_____

_____

_____

_____

_____

_____

What do you believe are the benefits of marriage for a woman?

_____

_____

_____

_____

_____

_____

What do you believe are the drawbacks of marriage for a woman?

_____

_____

_____

_____

_____

_____

_____

_____

_____

What differences do you notice in the male vs. female perceptions of pluses and minuses of marriage?

_____

_____

_____

_____

_____

_____

_____

_____

Are all "negatives" about marriage (e.g., lack of freedom) really losses or reasonable trade-offs?

_____

_____

_____

_____

_____

_____

_____

_____

Ask your husband what he has sacrificed for marriage.

_____
_____
_____
_____
_____
_____
_____
_____
_____

What have you sacrificed for marriage?

_____
_____
_____
_____
_____
_____
_____
_____
_____
_____

Do you believe the rewards of marriage are fair exchange for the sacrifices?

_____
_____
_____
_____
_____
_____
_____
_____
_____
_____
_____

Question 10: *What changes are you aware you should make to improve your marriage?*

1. "I should be more communicative with her and not get frustrated to the point that I don't talk to her when she doesn't act like I want or give me the approval that I seek."

2. "I am humble enough to realize that I'm not perfect and that growth is required. I must strive to keep our relationship alive and vibrant, because in twelve short years, our kids will be gone and we'll be all alone again. As I have grown in my spiritual walk, our bond has continually strengthened."

3. "I should affectionately touch her many times a day, look for ways to compliment her on a regular basis, be more appreciative, listen while cuddling without interrupting her, and try to support what she says without giving solutions. When talking, put down whatever, and look at her and touch her in a positive manner."

4. "I need to be more sensitive to my wife and try to be more romantic. Some of the mushy things don't mean much to some guys, but I know that women appreciate them. I'm going to try and reserve more energy to take her out more. I get tired and usually want to rest, but going out can be relaxing, too."

5. "Giving her more love, hugs, kisses. Hold my tongue more."

6. "I need to listen better to my wife, and not get impatient when she just wants to talk or vent. Listening without trying to solve the problem. Be there at the dinner table every night (which I hadn't thought about 'til reading your book)."

7. "To try to be more cognizant about helping my wife and showing her how much I love her and how much she means to me."

8. "I need to get out and have more 'guy' time with my boys and let her have a bit of a break. I want to spend more time with them anyway, so if she benefits, then it's a win-win for everyone."

9. "To make sure I stretch even further to think every minute what could I do to make her happy."

10. "To tell her what is going on with me and trust that she will listen."

11. "I need to do more acts of kindness."

12 "I need to be a stronger leader in our home, helping to plan and make sure the right things are happening. I need to anticipate more what needs to be done around the house and be able/willing to do it without being asked."

Your turn:

In what way(s) do you think that it is more difficult to be a man than a woman?

_____
_____
_____
_____
_____
_____
_____
_____
_____

In what ways do you think that it is more difficult to be a woman than a man?

_____
_____
_____
_____

What things about women do you think men will never "get"?

What things about men do you think women will never "get"?

What do you believe might be some basic incompatibilities between men and women?

_____
_____
_____
_____
_____
_____
_____

What do you think women need to "accept" about men that they can't/
shouldn't try to change?

_____
_____
_____
_____
_____
_____
_____
_____
_____
_____

What do you think men need to "accept" about women that they can't/
shouldn't try to change?

_____
_____
_____
_____
_____
_____
_____
_____

What is the "one thing" you wish your husband would forgive you for?

_____
_____
_____
_____
_____
_____
_____
_____
_____

What is the "one thing" you ought to forgive your husband for?

_____
_____
_____
_____
_____
_____
_____
_____

What do you believe are the significant impediments to peace in your marriage?

_____
_____
_____
_____
_____
_____
_____
_____
_____

What are you going to do about it?

_____

_____

_____

_____

_____

_____

_____

_____

_____

_____

Since men are not prone to wearing their emotions on their sleeves, nor are they generally as practiced or articulate about expressing their feelings as women are, hopefully this section served to give you greater insight into how men are emotionally impacted by their women's ways of behaving toward them. It is easy for a woman to "miss" her man's emotional state. We women are immersed in an emotionally intense and explicit world filled with other naturally verbal women, highly reactive children, and a deluge of female-oriented pop-psych-type women's magazines and television, all of which makes it all the more understandable that a man's more subtle, indirect style of communicating feelings might be overlooked and underestimated.

Rather than asking your man, "How do you feel?," you would be better served to notice his body language, facial expressions, level of joy and energy, and his willingness to be responsive to your requests, avoidant behaviors (TV, computers, work) to surmise there are "feelings" going on, and then ask him what he "needs" or "wants." Again, forget asking him what he is feeling; ask him what he is wanting. If you are open to the answer, it's better than blowing in his ear . . . unless, of course, that's what he's wanting!

PART FIVE
Proper Feeding:
Inspiration and Tips

Using Your **Woman Power!**

*All I ask of a woman is that she shall feel gently towards me
when my heart feels kindly towards her,
and there shall be the soft, soft tremor as of unheard bells between us.
It is all I ask.*
—D. H. LAWRENCE

I have been so incredibly moved and gratified with the response I've gotten from women who have read *The Proper Care and Feeding of Husbands* and have indeed discovered that they could and did transform their husbands, their marriages, and their lives into experiences of deep joy. These women have discovered their true power in the niceness of the feminine touch.

One such woman wrote:

"*Thank you. Thank you . . . I have been married for only ten months, but I can see how I needed this book ten years ago! I am in my early thirties and was brought up on the feminist platform rather than being taught the true power of a woman.*

"*I used to believe that to be powerful I had to fight—fight for my independence, respect, authority. Do you know where that got me? Lonely, scared, and angry. Looking back, I can see it was weakness, not strength, and a sense of victimhood, not power, that I was feeling. I didn't know how to be a woman.*

"*I have been applying what you taught me in your book, and what I have heard you say on your radio show. Weathering the big challenges of life as a couple is critical—but I now see that it is the small, everyday things that I believe can keep my marriage strong and loving.*

"*The small things I do for my husband now make such a difference—like getting up extra early so I can get him breakfast before I leave for work, telling him how proud I am of him, leaving hidden love notes for him to find, and taking care of myself so he knows I am proud to be his wife and I don't take that for granted.*

"*Sometimes his eyes fill up with tears and he tells me how grateful he is to have me as his wife. These small moments are the biggest moments to me. I never knew I could have such a strong impact on my husband.*

"*Thank you, Dr. Laura, for telling me how to better honor and take care of my husband. Thank you, Dr. Laura, for teaching me about the true power and responsibility of being a woman.*"

Only a few weeks after the release of *The Proper Care and Feeding of Husbands,* I put a question on my Web site, asking: "Based on reading *The Proper Care and Feeding of Husbands,* what specific changes did you make?" The prototypical answer was:

"*First of all, I've become more cheerful, less grumpy. I've quit nagging, catching myself with the urge and stopping myself*

before I speak. I've become more affectionate, hugging and kiss-
ing more and being more interested in lovemaking. I've started
complimenting more, expressing my gratitude for all his hard
work and for being such a great dad. I don't go on and on about
things that bother me anymore. I cook his favorite foods more
often. I've bought a few pieces of sexy underwear. I've tried
harder to control my PMS—the hardest thing, as it's like an
uncontrollable mood wave that turns me schizo."

The second part of the question had to do with short- and
long-term changes the reader noticed her husband making in
response to her "care and feeding":

"In response, he has been:
- *more helpful around the house*
- *more loving and affectionate*
- *calling to tell me he loves me*
- *asking what he can do for me*
- *complimenting me on my mothering and other things*
- *taking me out*

"As for the 'long-term,' I can't tell this soon, but I am confi-
dent that his love will grow (as will mine) and we will weather
storms more readily—and as a united team. Furthermore, our
kids are benefiting so much from seeing us this way. Less ten-
sion, grumpiness, resentment—more love, laughter, and team-
work."

Subjugation? Oppression? Loss of identity?   No. It's
WOMAN POWER. And see its majesty, benevolence, impact,
and blessing?

Here are a few quotes from women who, frankly, were
amazed at the impact of their WOMAN POWER:

"Then he called my office at 9 A.M. just to tell me he loved me.
*I was shocked! He had never, can I say **never** done that before.*
So, just changing a couple of things I do that were very easy to
do, changed a lot. My eight-year-old daughter asked why

Daddy was in such a good mood. I just smiled at her and told her, 'Because Mommy loves him.' "

Another:

"My husband's immediate response was (I'm ashamed to say), 'You're scaring me.' When I asked why, he replied, 'Because you're being nice to me . . . what's wrong?' Now it's been a few weeks and he is happier. He is less stressed. He is fun. He laughs more. He is more tolerant with our three teenagers. He (and I) gets a lot of sex!"

Another:

"We were very much in love before I read your book, but I clearly understood how I could easily neglect the small things in our relationship that truly mean the world to the love of my life. I am head over heels in love with my man all over again, and he and I are more whole as partners than we EVER have been before."

Another:

"I was more patient and showed him more affection, to the point where he isn't bugging me anymore about sex. Instead, he is saying he is worn out from all the lovemaking!"

Another:

"I had no idea men were so vulnerable—and it touches my heart. I had no idea that my behavior as a wife toward my husband is so vital to his emotional well-being. And I think it is so sweet that they want to be our heroes. You see, Dr. Laura, I guess I thought that a man's career and his role as the provider of the family already made him feel important. I never knew that a wife's acceptance and approval is so essential in making a

man feel VALUED. Knowing that my womanly love has such power, makes me feel so good to be a woman!"

And finally:

"I made the conscious decision to give my hubby ten minutes of uninterrupted time before dinner. Normally, he doesn't get more than a hug and kiss hello until after dinner. During those ten minutes, I didn't say boo about all my daily stress stuff (it no longer mattered to me if I won the 'who had the worst day' contest), I asked him how his day went, looked at a project that he was working on and gave comments as he requested, and said dinner would be ready in about a half hour. He came out of his home office BEFORE dinner was ready (normally I have to drag him away from his work to eat) and chatted and helped with setting the table and such. Now, THAT'S POWER! The reason I did these simple things is because you have been nagging about the woman having the power to set the tone in the house, and it's so totally true!"

Your turn:
What are your biggest concerns or worries about "changing"?

_____

_____

_____

_____

_____

_____

_____

_____

_____

_____

_____

What are your biggest concerns about your husband's reaction to your changes?

_____

_____

_____

_____

_____

_____

_____

_____

_____

What feelings do you hope you will lose/gain from your changes?

_____

_____

_____

_____

_____

_____

_____

_____

_____

What do you wish your husband would say to his friends about you, his wife, when you're not there?

_____

_____

_____

_____

_____

_____

_____

_____

_____

What are the special ways in which you believe your man needs "caring and feeding"?

_____

_____

_____

_____

_____

_____

_____

_____

_____

I recently had a call from a twenty-four-year-old woman, which epitomizes the main reason men are "hungry." She called because her boyfriend of four years has hurt her feelings. Of course he did.

To paraphrase the dialogue:

KATHY: He told me that if I went to dental school outside of the state he wouldn't marry me.

DR. LAURA: You mean, he doesn't want to marry someone who is going to be out of state for the first four years of his marriage?

KATHY: Yes. I just don't understand that. That's very hurtful.

DR. LAURA: You're kidding.

KATHY: No, I'm not. It's not necessarily in my control. The school in San Francisco hasn't let me know yet if they're accepting me. But if they don't, I'll have no choice.

DR. LAURA: Really? No choice?

KATHY: No.

DR. LAURA: You can't understand his concern, his feelings on this?

KATHY: No. We planned to get married.

DR. LAURA: What other plans do you have?

KATHY: Well, I figured get married after dental school, when I'm twenty-eight. Then I'd work for two years and have a child at thirty.

DR. LAURA: This is *your* schedule?

KATHY: Yes.

DR. LAURA: Well, you know, if you have sex enough times, regardless of birth control, you'll get pregnant. One cannot always time it.

KATHY: Oh, yes I will. I won't have a child until thirty.

DR. LAURA: How are you going to ensure that?

KATHY: Abstinence.

DR. LAURA: You expect this guy to marry you and not see you for four years and then be abstinent because your schedule rules? And, if he doesn't, he's an insensitive, selfish brute who is hurting your feelings. Yikes!

Unfortunately, this mentality runs pretty much through the upcoming wave of new wives and mothers. Clearly, "wife-ing" and "mothering" no longer hold any priority, even though they are still "wanted" experiences. The "wanted" part is that natural instinct to bond and nurture that is lovely and sweet about women. However, since we are so "evolutionarily advanced," it is easy to override what is natural with daycare (get somebody else to mother!) and the *im*proper care and feeding of husbands (how dare they get in the way of our self-actualization!).

There have always been women who were unable to be or uncomfortable being warm and loving to their men and children because of serious prior physical, mental, or sexual abuse, mental illness, addictions, bad role-modeling from parents, history of unfortunate relationships, and so forth. However, what is new is a patent disregard for the needs and feelings of children and husbands—which do not change with "the times." This, as I've pointed out, is the ugly by-product of a feminist-centered culture that has devalued what is truly meaningful (sacrifice, commitment, obligation, morality, loyalty) for immediate gratification and material gain, a bizarre notion of equality of the sexes, and power.

Having emotional independence, money, possessions, and position at the expense of emotional interdependence and obligations to one's family do not make a woman more powerful. Actually, it is a great and sad loss for women. That's why this book is titled *Woman Power*. We women need to take our power back from the ugly and seemingly invisible forces that pushed us back from what is ultimately meaningful and use that power to transform our men, our families, and our lives.

That, of course, does not mean we cannot have careers, jobs, hobbies, and other outside challenges. It does mean that we must not forget how we are the core thread in the tapestry of the family unit. When our outside challenges dominate, when we let the stresses dictate our moods and willingness to be caring and be giving, when we behave as though marriage and life in general is all about "us," when we are angry at the very blessing of our importance to our family, that tapestry unravels; and we women are not happier.

Women call me, feeling all of that. They speak of feeling confused and stuck. They have bought the notion of "balance" and don't know what to do when all the dishes fall off the balance sticks and crash on the floor. Balance is bull! I don't believe balance is the appropriate concept or philosophy. Balance generally means "do it all," and the stuff you don't actually get paid for comes last.

A healthy, happy, successful, more peaceful life punctuated with joy comes from making *choices*. When you come to a fork in the road, you don't "balance" by going back and forth between them, do you? No, you make a choice. And yes, choices leave something behind. When you bob your hair short, you can no longer put it up in a quick ponytail, can you? Some people look at choices as a bad thing for the very truth that something is left behind.

So many men have written me that when they marry they realize that they give up their single life of dating and fooling around with no obligation, which can be a lot of fun . . . for a while. When they take the other fork in the road, marital commitment, they express the joy and pride that comes from taking care of a wife and children; providing and protecting them, being leaders, heroes, role models to their children, lovers to their wives. The only time they are unhappy with that choice is when they are marginalized and dismissed by their wives. Yet, most men in that predicament will stay and suffer out of loyalty and obligation, and because that is what a "real man" would do.

There is no need for the epidemic level of marital misery today. We women have the power to make the difference. All power is a burden; all power comes with responsibility. However, remember that this power is a blessing that can bring forth even more blessings. The letters and transcribed calls for this part of the book are shared with you for motivation and inspiration. Prepare to be touched, challenged, moved, excited, and a little bit frightened. Why frightened? Well, if you've just gotten too used to the sad way things are in your marriage and your life, it may be difficult to imagine being comfortable with changes, choices, heightened communication, intimacy, and even happiness.

Well, girlfriend, tighten your seat belt, you've got an exciting ride ahead!

A NEW ATTITUDE

As I have already nagged, the most important factor dictating the quality of your mood, marriage, and life, is your "attitude." Attitude refers to your mind-set, way of thinking, your feelings and beliefs about something, which ultimately dictate your approach. Now, do you have to change your attitude before you can effectively use your WOMAN POWER? Yes, you do.

Why? Because when you filter everything through negativity, hostility, historical resentment, hurt, anger, and competitiveness, the only resulting vision is a sense of hopelessness and helplessness.

And you can't see, and therefore don't benefit from, the beauty that is there.

One reader decided to try a "new attitude":

"I have decided to be happy for my daily family 'chores' and have actually become happy to do them. Funny, how if you just change your mind-set, everything just falls into place. I now look for small ways to show my love by doing little things for him. I realized that he had been trying for months to please me but it was never good enough in my mind—that negative thinking you've discussed. I felt sorry for my poor husband for enduring my behavior all this time. And because of me, the whole family was unhappy and walking on eggshells.

"My husband is always ready to make love with me. I used to dread it but now I enjoy it. I am now gratified to know that he still desires me even with a little extra weight I have put on over the 13½ years of marriage . . . our children are happier lately because we are a happier couple. Once we seriously discussed divorce, and now it isn't even a thought. Thank you so very much for saving my marriage."

She "decided to be happy" about chores.

She "decided to see" the loving things he had been doing for her and the family.

She "decided to be enthusiastic" about lovemaking.

She now has a husband who speaks to her more sweetly, spends less time on the computer in the evenings, who calls her at work to tell her how beautiful she looked at dinner last night, who left a small stuffed animal on her pillow, took her to a matinee even though he hates crowds, helps her work on the backyard, and brags to people about her woodworking talents.

All because of a change in attitude. Whew!

Your turn:

Make a list of all the behaviors and traits your husband has which you see in the negative and try to come up with a positive "spin." (For example: He nit-picks. Perhaps it is because he is trying to be helpful and doesn't feel listened to. Perhaps he's just anxious about being perfect himself and needs to know that he's my hero just the way he is.) At first, this will be difficult to do. Don't worry about that. A change in attitude and a willingness to see things in a fresh and positive light when we've had the knee-jerk and habitual response of seeing in a negative light takes some practice.

_____

_____

_____

_____

_____

_____

_____

_____

_____

_____

_____

Another female reader had been absorbed in the attitude that "he" was the jerk and the reason "they" were not happy. After reading *The Proper Care and Feeding of Husbands* she realized that she shared the title of "jerk" with him!

> *"The worst thing was when I started to hear how my two boys spoke to my husband, and I realized that it only mirrored how I had been speaking to him. I was so ashamed. Like so many women who call your show, I thought that I deserved something for Valentine's Day just because I was the woman and I was the wife—no matter how jerky I was being.*
>
> *"I am happy to say that, after reading your book and doing what it says, for the first time in sixteen years of marriage, I*

woke up to a card and a present first thing in the morning. It was one of the happiest times in my life. Not because he bought me something, but because I knew I deserved it this year."

Your turn:

Think about how your behavior toward your husband guides the reactions of others toward him (children, friends, family).

_____

_____

_____

_____

_____

_____

_____

_____

_____

_____

_____

List five ways he's a jerk and five ways you're a jerk. Take just one of your jerk issues that you think might be interacting with a jerk issue of his—and see what happens when you change that in yourself. Give it a few days. What did you discover?

_____

_____

_____

_____

_____

_____

_____

_____

_____

_____

_____

Another wife wrote to me that her husband had already told her about her rotten attitude. She thought that it was a miracle that *The Proper Care and Feeding of Husbands* came out right after that sad event. She then realized that the many times he had openly rebuked her behavior wasn't a chastisement from "her dad," but a hurt husband's plea for respect in his own household.

> *"This wonderful, hardworking, intelligent, funny, strong leader and lover hasn't changed much since I met him. It was ME and my unreasonable expectations that clouded my vision of him. My bad attitude had really become ingrained and compulsive."*

She then related a few examples of what she described as her "evil way," which was to deflate his triumphant or happy moment by finding some negative that would highlight how "she is hurt" because, for example, of the time of the day he called to tell her about a promotion. She would lay guilt trips on him about everything.

One night, remembering the lessons in the book about attitude, she caught herself mid-nasty and turned the moment into a positive.

> *"That night I also snuck into the shower with him to show my real appreciation for his accomplishment . . . I didn't know sparks could fly in water!"*

Another wife realized that a bad attitude can be nurtured even when you're not speaking of your discontents out loud. In reading *The Proper Care and Feeding of Husbands,* she

> *". . . found myself feeling more compassion for my husband, and for men in general. My defensiveness disappeared. I had more energy. In two days [of her new attitude] he used the words, 'It feels like a honeymoon.' The best part is that after twenty-seven years of marriage, I am falling in love with my husband again.*
>
> *"Before reading your book, I would give myself a 90 percent*

as a wife. I was supportive and respectful, and did my nagging and criticizing in a journal to myself. I was tense and exhausted, and ate to relieve stress. Now I would give myself a 95 percent, because the desire to nag and criticize, even on paper, has gone. Just because I didn't say it, didn't mean it didn't affect him or me."

Your turn:

Check yourself for how much negative ruminating you do in your journal, your mind, with others. Each time those negative images come to mind, shift over immediately into a good thought or memory with him. Record a few of these instances and note how your feelings change.

_____

_____

_____

_____

_____

_____

_____

_____

_____

_____

_____

One engaged listener is somewhat panicked about getting married because of her own attitude.

"I am engaged but, for mainly financial reasons, will not be getting married for a year and a half. I have been stressing a bit about getting married, mainly because I am worried that my own relationship will eventually become like my parents'. I realize now that I am not a victim of the experiences I have seen thus far—the quality of my marriage will come primarily from choices I make! During this year and a half, I intend to read your book and learn how to maintain a harmonious relation-

*ship between my future husband and myself. I will make it a
habit to do nice things for him and show him how valuable he
is whether or not I 'feel like it.'* "

Your turn:

Please explore the attitudes about marriage, mothering, and "wife-ing" that
you got from your parents; positive and negative aspects. What are you having
to "learn" or "unlearn"? In what ways do you find yourself treating your man
unpleasantly based upon your early family experiences?

_____

_____

_____

_____

_____

_____

_____

_____

_____

_____

Another reader wrote me about the knee-jerk reaction of
her coworker to a friend who married a man from a more traditional culture. The irony of her coworker's criticisms compared with her own life's choices certainly highlighted an
important aspect of attitude: perspective.

> *"I remember a lady I worked with telling me she had a friend
> from college who married an Arab man, and she described how
> her friend was forced to cook his native food and she was not al-
> lowed to work.*
>
> *"Upon closer questioning, it turned out that her friend had
> a master's degree but was staying home to raise three young
> children until they reached school age, which was at her hus-*

band's request but was certainly something she was happy about.

"I thought about how disturbed this coworker was at her friend's lifestyle. Then I looked at my coworker's lifestyle, which included two kids by two different dads, both long gone, and she was working two jobs to support them. Who is oppressed?"

Your turn:

Think about what "classical, traditional male-female roles" you've had a bad attitude about and imagine your life within that picture. In what way would you imagine your life might be hurt ... or improved? What behaviors do you think you might even enjoy, were it not for societal negative views of traditional female-male roles?

_____

_____

_____

_____

_____

_____

_____

_____

_____

_____

_____

And now, for a levity break. One of my listeners sent me this Internet joke:

GREAT ADVICE FOR LADIES

If you want someone willing to make a fool of himself simply over the joy of seeing you ... buy a dog.

If you want someone who will eat whatever you put in front of him and never says it's not quite as good as his mother made it ... buy a dog.

If you want someone always willing to go out, at any hour, for as long and wherever you want . . . buy a dog.

If you want someone to scare away burglars without a lethal weapon that terrifies you and endangers the lives of your family and all the neighbors . . . buy a dog.

If you want someone who is content to get up on your bed just to warm your feet and whom you can push off if he snores . . . buy a dog.

If you want someone who will never touch the remote, doesn't care about football, and can sit next to you and watch a romantic movie . . . buy a dog.

If you want someone who never criticizes what you do, doesn't care if you are pretty or ugly, fat or thin, who acts as if every word you say is especially worthy of listening to, and loves you unconditionally, perpetually . . . buy a dog.

But, on the other hand,

If you want someone who will never come when you call,

Ignores you totally when you come home,

Leaves hair all over the place,

Walks all over you,

Runs around all night,

Only comes home to eat and sleep,

And acts as if your entire existence is solely to ensure his happiness,

Then, my friend,

Buy a cat!

Your turn:
Please think about all the expectations and demands you make on your husband's attitude and behaviors REGARDLESS of how "cared and fed" he is by you. Think about what you can do to care and feed him into the mind-set that will get many of these expectations met.

_____

_____

_____

_____

_____

_____

_____

_____

_____

_____

Mandy, a recent caller, had a question for me unrelated to *The Proper Care and Feeding of Husbands.* However, she began the conversation by telling me that the book had changed her life forever. I couldn't resist asking her how that was so. The discussion, having a lot to do with attitude, was humbling and moving. I'd like to share it with you.

MANDY: Before your book we were going to get divorced.
DR. LAURA: Really?!
MANDY: I didn't know what to do. I had a total lack of knowledge, and before your book I just gave up. I didn't know what else to do. And then, after he got me the book, I read it and . . . I'm kissing his feet every single day.

DR. LAURA: What did you come to understand after reading the book that you believe you didn't know before?

MANDY: Well, just the fact of what my role as wife is, and also how very simple and basic men really are, and that women make the mistake of making them so complicated. As soon as I realized that, my hackles came down, I stopped challenging him all the time, and everything has been wonderful.

DR. LAURA: So, you're basically saying it was an attitude shift.

MANDY: Attitude shift, absolutely. One hundred percent.

DR. LAURA: If you had to give one word to describe your attitude before the book and then after, what would the two words be?

MANDY: Before—selfish. After—grateful.

DR. LAURA: Grateful for what?

MANDY: Because he's an awesome man. He works so hard. He doesn't do any of the goofy stuff and he treats me wonderfully.

DR. LAURA: And why do you think you didn't see that before the book?

MANDY: Because I think I expected too much, and I was just self-indulgent. I expected him to be romantic every day. And it wasn't right. I should not have expected stuff like that. You know, I have to give in order to receive. And I needed to give freely and genuinely, and I wasn't doing that.

DR. LAURA: And why do you think you weren't?

MANDY: Probably a prelearned way of dealing with men that I learned from my mother. I always felt that she didn't respect my dad, she didn't appreciate how hard he worked. I think that passed down to me.

DR. LAURA: Now, when he gave you the book, considering the attitude you had then, why were you willing to read it?

MANDY: I was still open to fixing things, even though I had gone to the extent of wanting a divorce. There was still a part of me that was praying something would happen, that would fix it.

The first thing I thought when he gave me the book, the first thing I thought of was if this is full of tradition and how to be submissive and stuff, I'm throwing this book in the garbage! And (laughs) when I started to read it, it was not like that at all. It was wonderful and your words were so simple, so basic, and yet so many women don't understand that.

DR. LAURA: I appreciate you saying that, and I'm glad it saved these little kidlets from a broken home.

MANDY: Oh, so am I.

See? A new attitude works!

In order to work on her attitude, another reader made a quick comparison list of the disparate ways that she and her husband were dealing with the normal, natural issues of marriage. She was chagrined at her own list.

My Husband	*I*
looks for intimacy	*find excuses not to*
works really hard to provide for family	*focus on my own busy self*
gives me presents	*complain / exchange for something else*
tries to plan things for the family	*nag / dismiss, try to be always right*
tells me I'm beautiful	*wear raggedy clothes; don't shave legs or try to look pretty*

"That is a sampling of the THEN. Happily, I am pleased to have transformed into the NOW. After an evening of inti-

macy recently, my husband made this comment: 'Wow, you seem so motivated.' My response: 'I'm on a mission.' He smiled and went to bed with a silly grin on his face.

"The other day as he was washing the dishes, I snuck up behind him and said, 'When you wash the dishes, you turn me on.' He vowed to wash dishes 365 days of the year."

Your turn:

Spend some time thinking about the *absolute description* of any "disturbing event or interaction" you've had with your husband, and the *subjective interpretation* you gave the situation (which is what ultimately depresses you). For example—he does/doesn't do something and you "interpret" it as mean, uncaring, selfish, vengeful, insensitive, and so forth. Could it just be an innocent act without all those connotations? Spend a week looking for these moments and record them here.

_____

_____

_____

_____

_____

_____

_____

_____

_____

_____

APPRECIATION: SEEING THAT YOU'VE ALREADY STRUCK GOLD!

"He is my hero, my lover, my best friend, but more important, he is my husband.

"Thank you for opening my eyes, Dr. Laura, and giving me the vision to see what I had all along!"

An attitude change does help you to embrace new ways of seeing and enjoying your role as a wife. Positive attitude changes increase possibilities for inner peace and mutual happiness. The next stage of your journey is to realize that without doing a thing, you've already passed GO and collected $200; your husband is just brimming with gifts.

As one reader wrote:

"I have learned to appreciate the little things that my husband does, even if it is something so small as taking something out of the freezer for dinner. I find myself noticing the small, helpful things that he does, rather than only noticing the mistakes I think he makes."

Your turn:

Make a list of five typical criticisms you frequently communicate to your husband.

_____

_____

_____

_____

_____

_____

_____

_____

_____

_____

Make a list of five typical compliments about "small things" you frequently communicate to your husband.

_____
_____
_____
_____
_____
_____
_____
_____
_____

Decide which of the criticisms really need to be said . . . are they really important enough to keep bringing up? Really?

_____
_____
_____
_____
_____
_____
_____
_____
_____

The criticisms you believe are necessary to bring up: After five days of compliments without those criticisms, see which of the criticisms still seem important, and which have been appropriately dealt with by your husband without you bringing constant attention to them.

_____
_____
_____
_____
_____

Another listener offered:

"I thought I had a good marriage—not perfect, but strong, steady, and outlasting in-law problems, a teenage daughter, a deadbeat ex-husband, a move across country, and a multitude of other issues of life. My husband doesn't gamble, drink or use drugs; quit smoking years ago, is an active parent, has a wonderful work ethic, would NEVER even think of raising a hand to me, is as faithful to his wedding vows as they come, and lets me have 175-pound potbellied pigs in the house.

"So, why am I such a witch? I never gave him any credit for all the daily wonderful things he did for me, for us. I would make snide jokes about him when people complimented him to me. After reading your book, I quit focusing on ME and what I need and want, and complaining about what he doesn't do. Then, I began being grateful for what he does do and thinking about his needs. It works. We're both happier."

Your turn:
What do you believe has made it difficult for you to show your husband how much you appreciate all that he does do?

What change(s) have you noticed in your husband when you start complimenting him on the "small stuff"?

_____

_____

_____

_____

_____

_____

_____

_____

_____

_____

_____

Another listener shared with me a copy of a list she made of her "life's blessings" after she came to the realization that she wasn't appreciating full what she had in front of her.

"I realized I was feeding my useless anger by focusing on what I don't like about my life, instead of appreciating all the blessings I do have."

Counting My Blessings

1. My husband's love, intelligence, loyalty, and sense of humor
2. The love, beauty, and spirit of my daughter
3. The love, kindness, and strength of my son
4. The devotion, enthusiasm, and humor of my two close friends
5. My sister-in-law's sweetness and moral conviction
6. My good health
7. Financial security
8. My daily walk, up and down canyons, with Torrey Pines, and the Pacific nearby
9. Singing along to country music

10. *Finding an excellent book and reading it*
11. *Enjoying movies with my husband*
12. *Following current events*
13. *Cooking and eating delicious food*
14. *Creating and living in a beautiful home*
15. *Snuggling in a comforter by the fire with my husband, kids, and dog*
16. *Listening to the* Dr. Laura Show
17. *Embracing the gift of life*
18. *Appreciating God's presence in our lives*

Your turn:

No one is denying that there are painful, difficult, unfortunate occurrences in everyone's life. Yet, the quality of life doesn't depend on that list . . . it depends largely on how you respond to those challenges. One of the basic aspects of a good attitude about marriage is a more philosophical response to life in general. Please take the time to write down your blessings. Review this list every day—especially when you feel like a bad mood is coming on!

_____

_____

_____

_____

_____

_____

_____

_____

_____

_____

_____

_____

_____

_____

_____

_____

It is a beautiful thing when a woman discovers that her problem is not "men," but her *men*tality about men. When a woman lets go of her unnecessary anger, a beautiful thing happens, as the next reader reveals:

> "*I love our newfound love affair, and all it took was a small change in attitude from me.*
>
> "*All my years growing up I was raised to hate and distrust men in general, my father in particular. I didn't have any male role models to show me the 'true man' image. Here was my husband, trying his best to show me, and all I did was ignore, belittle, disrespect, and focus on myself. Thank you, thank you, for this 'new attitude.'*"

It is too easy to get crass and ignore the value of what your man gives you. Another reader wrote:

> "*I was not verbally abusive, demanding, demeaning, or particularly whiny. But I was not full of praise, encouragement, affirmation, or gratefulness, either. My indifference to his accomplishments (the things 'he was supposed to do') left my husband feeling unmotivated. Then, the more he allowed things to go to pot around the house, the more moody, unnecessary, and ineffective he began to feel. His feelings of being unimportant and ineffective at home led to a brief affair.*
>
> "*Instead of freaking out about the affair, I found myself recognizing that, while it was my husband's decision in the end to step outside of our marriage, I had played a definitive role in making it possible for him to make that decision. My actions and attitudes toward my husband had helped plant the seed of a choice to be even made when this other woman presented herself to him.*
>
> "*I realized that I had not been properly caring for and feeding my husband. I waited for him to come home the night I discovered the affair, and I confronted him. I prayed for God to grant me the peace, wisdom, and self-control necessary to handle the conversation and whatever it may bring RATIONALLY. I*

thought before I spoke, did not fall into the quicksand of 'reaction.' And I was able to greet everything my husband had to say with love and understanding. For the next three or four hours, my husband and I had the best, deepest conversation we had had since probably before we got married.

"My husband has since told me that hearing my expression of his importance to my life, witnessing my grace under pressure, and the emotional maturity with which I approached him that night, were the final nails in the affair's coffin."

She described the next weeks as a commitment to honor her husband and discover her self. She prayed to God to give her husband a new wife, and to let it be her! She didn't wait until she "felt like it" to make the changes that were necessary to keep her marriage alive.

"I started finding and doing things, those things my husband needs in order to feel admired and appreciated. And, instead of pulling out my bag of tricks only for special occasions, I reach into it at least once a day. And IT IS FUN!! Dr. Laura, I am having so much fun GIVING to my husband. It makes me feel like the wife I have always wanted to be—the wife I so wrongly believed was my husband's responsibility to tap into with his actions and attitudes. And, this, in turn, is bringing out the husband I always knew he was."

Your turn:
Please consider some unpleasant, bad behavior of your husband's. Try to see if it is a reaction to the demoralization a man feels when his woman doesn't think he's her hero.

_____

_____

_____

_____

_____

IT'S NOT ALL ABOUT YOU!

"I have a perfect marriage, so why would I need this book? With your guidance, I turned the searchlight inward and began to look at myself from a new perspective—my husband's. I began to hear myself through his ears and see myself through his eyes. EEEEKK!!! When I so smugly said, 'I have a good marriage,' I wasn't looking at it from my husband's viewpoint.

"If asked, would he say the same? Maybe, but most likely he wouldn't use words like 'fulfilling,' 'safe,' 'exciting,' or 'satisfying,' as I would. He might use adjectives like 'stressful,' 'insecure,' 'frigid,' or 'mundane.' How sad is that? Time for a wakeup call!! I bought your book immediately!!!"

Frankly, I've been somewhat surprised and very impressed by the loving sensitivity that so many women have expressed by their willingness to "see the other side" and admit to their own lapses in acknowledging and caring about the well-being of their husbands.

Mostly, they admit to the one-sidedness behind the nagging and whining which pretty much defined their marital persona: One wife wrote the following (excerpted) Valentine's Day letter to her husband after reading *The Proper Care and Feeding of Husbands*, which helped her to see that a marriage involves two, not just one and an adjunct: the husband.

"To my loving, wonderful husband, Alex:

These past few weeks I have realized how much you love me in your own little, unique ways. Thank you for helping me with our kids—bathing, feeding, playing, teaching them right and wrong despite working so hard at the night shift, sleeping less hours in order to spend time with them. Thank you for being a hands-on dad.

"You have showered me with love every single day, especially from the day our son was born. I have neglected to appreciate everything that you do and did for me. I now know that when you take out the kids so I can sleep during the day it is your way of saying, 'I love you very much, honey!' These words are not so strong compared to all the things you have done for me in the name of love.

"There are a lot of examples of things you do for me and tell me how much you love me—every day is Valentine's Day when I'm with you. Thanks for being such a good provider, for all your hard work and sacrifices in order to have our finances in the ++++. You've put up with all my destructive behaviors in the past, and I don't think all the chocolate cake I bake in your whole lifetime is enough to make up for it."

Acknowledging how you have hurt your husband, by commission or omission, is a great first step and an unbelievably liberating one. Too many people have trouble saying "I'm sorry," and that is such a shame. For it is in that humbling moment that the other's compassion and love is ignited. When you "own up to" your mistakes, ill-deeds, selfish behaviors, or even admit to what you "didn't know," your husband is not feeling triumphant over you; he is feeling your tenderness towards him. Such an admission is a love offering, really. Frankly, my dears, he will melt.

Your turn:
Please make a list, based on reading *The Proper Care and Feeding of Husbands* and your work so far, of the ways you now see and accept that you have been thinking and behaving in a one-sided manner in your marriage (your problems, your pain, your disappointments, your hurts, your feelings, your family, your desires . . .) and have not given equal weight to his.

_____

_____

_____

_____

_____

_____

_____

_____

Please write to your husband a letter of apology and acknowledgment of where you have let him down, not considered his viewpoint, feelings, needs, etc. When you feel ready, please give it to him, wrapped in a bow.

_____

_____

_____

_____

_____

_____

_____

_____

You may be thinking, "Well, I don't know, I don't think he's been upset. He hasn't said anything." Oh, yes he has. But if your radio receiver is turned off, all the beautiful classical music being sent through the airwaves will never be registered as having happened!

One woman wrote:

> *"I feel that your book is simple and sensible. It's not as though you've invented this new way to be a woman. You've just reminded us all that being a woman who wants and needs her man is a good and honorable thing.*

*"We've had our ups and downs, like every couple, but lis-
tening to you has let me relive all those things I did and said
over the years; things that I know hurt my husband. He never
said he was hurt, because that's just not what men do, but looking back I know he showed it in a myriad of ways that I chose
to ignore. I remember when he said that he wanted to help me
and do things for me. He actually said, years ago, 'Just pretend
that you need me a little bit. I know you can do things for
yourself, but I'd like to feel that I'm needed.'"*

The painful irony is that she was diagnosed with multiple
sclerosis in June of 2001. She wrote that they were sitting in
their front yard one day when she was feeling particularly
frightened and quite ill. He looked at her and simply said, "I'm
not going anywhere. I'll be right here."

*"I look forward to tomorrow as my jumping-off point for my
future as my man's woman. He is honorable, strong, funny, and
warm, and the best friend and husband I could wish for. Thanks
for helping me to remember that."*

It is so sad to me that so many women misconstrue "love"
and "interdependency" as "control." Not letting a man dominate
and control has been the paranoid mantra of the heterophobic
women's movement for decades. Perfectly reasonable women
imagine that letting him even have an opinion about what his
wife is doing is proof of his malevolency. Too sad for words.

Another woman wrote that her response to reading *The
Proper Care and Feeding of Husbands* was to

*". . . make him feel like part of this family, where I realize I did
not really include him before. It is sad when I think of what he
must have felt, the way I treated him. I never really thought
about it when I was doing that. I just carried on in this busy
life, and left no feelings for him. Life was the kids, work, responsibilities.*

"He is much more responsive to me now. He comes home from work earlier. He calls to say hello. He is more eager to tell me about his day and to hear about mine. We seem to be connecting at a different level. I have spent too many years making him feel lousy, but I can tell this will be a good thing in the long run. I would never have guessed that a book with this information would be able to change us so much. We have been to therapy many times and have never, ever had something as simple as this suggested to us."

Your turn:

Please examine in what ways you make your husband feel like you really need him. What are those ways and how do you let him know?

_____

_____

_____

_____

_____

_____

_____

_____

Please examine the ways in which you push your husband away when he tries to be "helpful." What are the feelings you're having that cause you to do that (example: you feel criticized, insecure, etc.)

_____

_____

_____

_____

_____

_____

_____

_____

What can you do now to show your husband that his input and presence are valued and desired?

_____

_____

_____

_____

_____

_____

_____

_____

_____

_____

_____

_____

There are, of course, early-life experiences that make it seem too difficult to see past your own hurts and fears. One woman wrote me that it took three readings of *The Proper Care and Feeding of Husbands* before she was willing and able to look at the positive virtues of her husband! Her first image was of him meeting her when she weighed three hundred pounds and telling her that he'd support her in her weight loss no matter what. However, losing the weight did not help her self-focus, because the weight was about being unattractive to men and an avoidance of sex as a response to her incestuous childhood experiences with her father.

"Finally, I was able to become compassionate and had to remind myself that this is my husband, and NOT my dad who abused me. It is OK to have sex—it is a duty of a wife who must please her husband. To my surprise, my husband came home last night and asked me to have sex more often than twice a year. For the first time, I listened and did not give him any excuses. And, for the first time, I was totally open, relaxed, and not uptight about having sex. To my surprise, I enjoyed sex for

*the first time in my life. I am looking forward to buying a nice
negligee to surprise my husband, and I promised myself to stay
focused on the present and to have more sex with my mate."*

Your turn:

What childhood or early-adult experiences of yours seem to be the "excuse"
for not staying focused on the present with your husband?

_____

_____

_____

_____

_____

_____

_____

_____

_____

_____

In what way(s) do you believe your "self-focus" is about protecting yourself
or taking out historical rage/hurt/fears on your husband?

_____

_____

_____

_____

_____

_____

_____

_____

_____

_____

I am sorry to say that I have spoken to too many brats on my radio program. I hope I've helped each one of them turn their eyeballs outward, so they can see more than just their own selfish desires being realized.

One such woman called with her husband. She is thirty-eight, and he is thirty-four. They have been married five years and have no children. This is her second marriage and his first. The problem is that, for the second time now, her friends have won some sort of contest and got cheap tickets to go hang out in New York City, and invited her along. Sounds reasonable, doesn't it? He even admitted feeling selfish for being negative about her going this second time, because he was "jealous." You see, they haven't been able to afford a vacation together yet, and he'd like to go to New York with her.

> KARA: I want to go. I'm not gonna lie about it, but I don't understand why he wouldn't be happy I would get something like that. I would, in turn, if he wanted to go on some kind of trip with somebody, I would support it. I believe he's jealous that I have the opportunity to go, because he's never been, and this will be my second time. And I also believe he's jealous because I have the friends who offer these things to me and he doesn't.
>
> RONALD: It's the jealousy that is not a fidelity issue. It's a lot like kids and Disneyland, and she gets to go and I don't get to go.
>
> DR. LAURA: Do you guys ever travel with each other?
>
> KARA: Well, we haven't taken a true vacation since we've been married, just because financially. . . .

It was at this point that I asked Ronald to hang up the phone. When I am going to "smack someone upside the head" I don't like their spouse to hear it . . . my notion of letting somebody save face.

DR. LAURA: I listened very carefully. You seem to dismiss his feelings about having a special vacation in New York with you. You've not put your money together to do something together. You seem to dismiss his feelings about this. Men are not generally as articulate about expressing feelings as we are, and so sometimes we have to take a leap from what they're saying to what they're meaning.

I don't think it would be smart for your marriage for you to do this. And I don't think it's about him pouting because you have friends who would cough up the dough. Think more deeply about this, Kara. I think it makes him feel inadequate that he cannot afford to do this for you and with you. And I think it makes him feel bad that every time you travel it's with your girlfriends and not him. And I think it makes him feel bad that you don't seem to care about his desires for the both of you. You're acting like a teenager whose parents are standing in the way of your fun—not like a wife who is supposed to be thinking of "we" and not just "me."

So frankly, if you care about your marriage, you will wait a day or two and then say to him something like, "You know, honey, I already went to New York without you, it was a blast to be able to do that, but, you know, we have never gone away together in the five years we've been married, so let's sit down and plot and plan our time to go to New York. Let's save the money and do it together. I love you."

I think that would be what a loving wife and a smart woman who wants to stay married would say.

Friends, I have no idea if she followed through on my advice or not. But millions of other women overheard that conversation and, hopefully, thought twice and then thrice about doing what they wanted to do simply because they could . . . and thought they simply had the right to, because, after all, they're independent women!

Your turn:

Think of the time(s) you sounded just like Kara—thinking that you should be able to do whatever you choose because your husband should not ever have any control or say over your actions. Think then about what feelings were going through his heart.

_____

_____

_____

_____

_____

_____

_____

_____

_____

_____

I was deeply gratified by the following letter from a woman married for eight years, with three children, who described herself as never knowing the proper way to treat a husband because she came from a home without a dad. She had no example of how a wife was supposed to be, other than from magazines, TV, and girlfriends with bad attitudes and bad marriages (they tend to go hand-in-hand).

She started out her letter admitting that:

"I treated my husband like he had no feelings—just because he didn't show them like I do. I never cared about his hard day, because MINE was harder. I never told him he was an important part of our family. I never told him I appreciate him going to work every day without complaint, to support our family so I could stay home and raise our kids. I put our kids before him. The only thing I ever told him was my complaints about feeling

like a slave: cooking, cleaning, doing laundry, etc. He was my trash can for dumping all my feelings into.

"I thought my husband wanted to 'get some' all the time. Why didn't he understand ME feeling too tired or not in the mood. Again—all about MY feelings, not his, because he didn't have feelings.

"In conclusion, I thought that my husband wasn't giving ME what I wanted out of a marriage, but it was because I wasn't giving him anything. I am getting everything I have always wanted now, because I gave my husband the respect, acceptance, and appreciation he deserved. It was so simple."

Your turn:

Give some consideration to those instances where you are so immersed in your own "pity party" that you discount his feelings or needs as an imposition.

_____

_____

_____

_____

_____

_____

_____

_____

_____

Give consideration to the circumstance where you put your own "pity party" aside and tend to your husband's feelings, needs, desires. Do you feel better or worse?

_____

_____

_____

_____

_____

MEN HAVE PROBLEMS, TOO!

A woman wrote to me that the fun in her marriage had faded, and they'd become the typical grumpy couple. At first, she didn't want to read *The Proper Care and Feeding of Husbands,* because she was uncomfortable finding out there was something for her to learn. Then, after listening to my readings of letters from "satisfied customers" on the air, she bought it and read it on the sly, because she didn't want him to "expect" anything.

She describes her husband as a pilot, by trade and by blood. But, about two years ago, he voluntarily gave up the cockpit, because it appeared that he was in danger of being laid off, and a nonflying aviation position became available. If he didn't make the switchover now, his next pilot position could be somewhere across the country. Together, they decided it was more important for their son to have a stable home with grandparents close by than for the husband to be physically in the cockpit.

"The other day my husband had a rough day at work. As a result, he was deeply missing the excitement of being in the cockpit and was dreading the next twenty or so years of 'flying a desk.' He commented to me, 'You have everything you wanted—to be home with the kids, a nice house. I had to give up the one thing I worked all my life to do.'

"Prior to reading your book, my response might have been something like, 'Before we got married, you agreed that you'd provide the income, and I'd be home with the kids. No job is perfect. You'll just have to stick it out with this one, because I'm not moving again. Our son deserves to grow up in one place.'

"This time, however, I recognized his end of the deal. He's right. I have everything I always wanted: a nice home, a great kid, a husband who responsibly goes to work every day, and the *ability to determine my own daily schedule. He has to go to an office and do what the boss tells him to do, and be there every day whether he feels like it or not.*

"The 'boy' I married had turned into a 'man.' Now I needed to be the woman he deserves. We spent a lot of time that evening talking about the job in general and discussing ways to handle the particular situation he had encountered that day. The next day I called him at work and he was much more relaxed. Things were much better, and he was glad I had thought about him.

"You say, Dr. Laura, that we women have the power to change our husbands, but I'm not seeing much change in mine. Perhaps that's because he really didn't need to change. I did. I'm able to let go more; I'm able to talk to my husband as an equal rather than as a counselor or mother. And I'm happier for it. I find him much more attractive than I have in years, because the admiration is returning to my attitude. And the more I admire him, the more he respects himself."

Your turn:
Please think about what your husband is sacrificing for you and the family—something that he loves and misses. Can you find a way to incorporate that back into your lives? If not, can you think of a way to make him feel better about it?

I particularly liked a brief letter from a wife and mother who realized that she was treating her husband as though he were a machine. She expected that the minute he got home from work he should do something around the house. She would nag, insult, demand, criticize, and generally hurt his feelings.

> *"After I read three chapters of* The Proper Care and Feeding of Husbands, *it hit me like a ton of bricks! It is because of his efforts that I get to be nurse, teacher, friend, and, most of all, mommy to our four children. It is because of his sacrifices that I haven't worked outside our home for twelve years.*
>
> *"That night, after he returned home from ten hours of his physically demanding job, I greeted him at the door and encouraged our children to do the same. While I was making dinner, he was watching TV. Our eleven-year-old said, 'Mom, is Dad going to watch TV all night?' (I wonder where he got that from?) I said, 'Why not? Daddy worked hard all day and that is how he wants to relax. Just like how you like to ride your bike when you get home from school.'*
>
> *"The look on my husband's face was wonderful. Was I actually defending his right to 'chill' for a while?*
>
> *"That next night he came home from work and finished a project I had been hounding him to do for two years! I didn't even say a word! He even bathed the kids and rubbed my shoulders while I did the dishes. Thank you, Dr. Laura, for encouraging—OK, insisting—that I give my husband the attention, affection, and appreciation that he so much deserves."*

When you acknowledge, and even defend, your husband's personhood and entitlement to moods and moments, it makes him more comfortable inside himself, and more cozy beside you!

One woman's husband has been suffering from depression due to losing the company which he had built up for over twenty years. There had been many hurts, financial and personal, over the past five or six years. These setbacks caused their lives to spin out of control, and they turned away from each other physically and emotionally.

> *"We pretty much lived as roommates, wrapped up in our own personal turmoil. The business loss was the major reason for his depression, but after reading your book, I realized that I had not supported him or even been affectionate with him as I used to be before the problems. I am so ashamed of myself for my behavior these last years."*

After reading *The Proper Care and Feeding of Husbands* she started using her WOMAN POWER. She apologized to him for not being the loving, affectionate wife she used to be and for not supporting him and being his cheerleader when he most needed it. She started smiling, hugging, and kissing him.

> *"I realize he is suffering so much pain beyond just our relationship, but this wonderful man I married has started blossoming again, and I can see him coming back to life. He is laughing and more playful, and he is smiling back at me and even reaches for me to give him a hug. WOW, Dr. Laura, I can't thank you enough. I am having so much fun thinking of things to do for him!*
>
> *"Please let wives out there know that our men may be facing battles in the business world and that they, being the protectors, don't always share their war stories. They may be dealing with so much more than we could ever know. They still need our love, affection, and a warm, welcoming home to retreat to.*
>
> *"Dr. Laura, I thank God and you for helping to save my marriage."*

Your turn:
Please think about the situations that you can imagine hurt or stress your husband. While you can't necessarily solve the problem for him, think about what care-taking you can do, what use of your WOMAN POWER could make him feel safe, hopeful, and like the champion again.

_____

_____

_____

_____

_____

_____

_____

_____

_____

Another wife came to the realization that when her husband talked about his stressful day, she would only half-listen, interrupting him to ask him to take out the trash or pour the milk for dinner. She always felt that his work stress really didn't have anything to do with their real life. She had to admit also to speaking to him with a "mommy tone" of condescension.

After reading *The Proper Care and Feeding of Husbands,* she greeted him at the door dressed like a wife, not a mommy, and with a hug and kiss. As it turned out, it had been one of his most stressful days. He was surprised when she said to their children as they interrupted their conversation, "Daddy and I are talking, and I'll help you when we are finished." He was stunned. She listened to him as he described his entire day, and it felt good to her. She could see the stress leave him because he was able to share it with her. After they talked, she told him to take some time to relax as she prepared dinner.

> *"I did all of this because I wanted to. What a revelation. For the first time in a very long time, my husband felt valued by me and I felt valuable to him. What is most amazing to me is that I am not making changes because of the rewards it will afford me, but because I love this man more deeply, more completely, and I see him more clearly now. I actually see him."*

Your turn:

Please list the ways in which, you imagine, your husband sees you as valuable to him.

_____

_____

_____

_____

_____

_____

_____

_____

_____

_____

Please list the ways in which you see your husband as valuable to you.

_____

_____

_____

_____

_____

_____

_____

_____

_____

Please examine how, when something bad happens in/out of the family/relationship that impacts both of you, you go into your own corner. Try coming out of that corner the very next time that happens and record the difference in yourself and your husband.

_____

_____

_____

_____

What can I say? He's a guy!

"There is something that your new book has made so clear to me—I HAD NO IDEA MEN WERE SO VULNERA-BLE!—and it touches my heart. Nor did I know that we had so much power over them as their wives!! WOW! What a concept. I knew that men need us to take care of them, but I always saw that in a more practical sense; like ironing their shirts and having dinner ready for them. But I had no idea that my behavior as a wife toward my husband is so vital to his emotional well-being. And I think it is so sweet that they want to be our heroes!

"You see, Dr. Laura, I guess I thought that a man's career and his role as the provider of the family already made him feel important. I never knew that a wife's acceptance and approval is so essential in making a man feel VALUED. Knowing that my womanly love has such power makes me feel so good to be a woman, a woman with a newfound respect for masculinity. Take that, feminists! It is such a shame that those feminist-types cannot see masculinity and femininity as the wonderful and sacred entities that they are."

Accepting your man for who and what he is is a gift of pure love. It is so very sad when a woman marries a man she considers "a work in progress." One of my listeners described an acquaintance of hers who has a husband similar to my listener's. The acquaintance is divorcing her husband, because she cannot accept him as he is. He's a good man, a faithful husband, a good provider, quite attractive, with many good qualities . . . but he's not perfect, either. Seems that all she focuses on are his faults.

> *"He is so hurt and grieving, because she was never happy with him as he was, always wanting to change him and have him meet her needs. Every time she complains about things he's done, I see that my husband has done similar things—but I was just able to accept that's how he is and not be offended.*
>
> *So many times in our marriage I know I could have held a grudge, gotten angry with him, rejected his advances, put him down, criticized him—but that's not what love is about."*

One of my single-but-engaged listeners got this insight while reading *The Proper Care and Feeding of Husbands*. She was appalled reading the stories of so many unhappy husbands. She was amazed at how the solutions and ideas presented were so simple to implement. It helped her come to an important realization during the planning for their wedding, the most important thing in her life at the moment, where everything had to be perfect! She realized that to him it was just a big party where he had to wear a tux, *". . . and, oh yeah, he's getting hitched."* She stopped nagging and complaining to him about his not being absolutely engrossed in choosing roses over orchids, or gold accents over silver.

> *"Like you said in the book and on your show many times, 'He's a GUY!'—and if I'd wanted a guy interested in flowers, I should be marrying a florist!*
>
> *"I plan to be the best wife and life partner I can be for him. I also plan to keep this book on my bookshelf forever, and will refer to it when times are tough. Because even though my mom raised me to believe the mantra, 'I am woman, hear me roar!' after implementing just a few common courtesies so many women forget to give their loved ones ('please,' 'thank you,' 'I love you'), my new mantra is 'I AM HIS WOMAN, hear me purrrrrr!'"*

Your turn:
Please list all the qualities of your husband you are dissatisfied with.

_____

_____

_____

_____

_____

_____

_____

_____

Please relist all the qualities of your husband that you are dissatisfied with, which you knew were his qualities before you married him.

_____

_____

_____

_____

_____

_____

_____

_____

Please explain why you're mad that the man you picked is the man you picked.

_____

_____

_____

_____

_____

_____

_____

_____

Please list all the qualities of your husband that annoy you that simply are typical "guy" behavior.

_____

_____

_____

_____

_____

_____

_____

_____

Please list all the qualities your husband has to deal with that are simply typical "gal" behavior.

_____

_____

_____

_____

_____

_____

_____

_____

Please discuss what you've learned from answering these last five questions.

_____

_____

_____

_____

_____

_____

_____

_____

One reader wrote that *The Proper Care and Feeding of Husbands* taught her a couple of important things. She explained that she and her husband are extremely opposite in temperament: she is Type A, he is a laid-back Type B. What she didn't realize, though, is that she never once had considered how his Type B-ness affects him.

"He needs time to relax. A day off for a Type B guy mostly involves watching TV and scratching himself. During this last vacation, I had him spend every single day working in some way: on the cars, on the house. I thought nothing of it. When I get time off, I look for projects. I never considered how miserable this would make him.

"My first change was to be more considerate of his need for time to do absolutely nothing. In fact, one day I left a 'Get Well' card on the armoire, saying that I appreciate all of his work during his vacation, and now he needed to recover. On his bedside table was a thermal carafe full of freshly brewed, freshly ground coffee, and a mug. Next to a chair was a big gift bag full of goodies: a DVD he'd mentioned wanting to see, bags of junk food, magazines, almonds, candy bars . . . a big bag full of guilty pleasures. I instructed him to stay in bed all day and do nothing!

He was thrilled. He must have called me at work to thank me ten times that day. I can't even explain how good it made me feel to know that I had done such a little thing and made him so truly happy."

She also bought some sexy lounging outfits to look nice for him. However, he told her that his favorite outfit is when she's wearing just her wedding ring. Whoa!

Your turn:
Please come up with some plan to positively acknowledge your husband's unique personality qualities—especially in an area you have been feisty about.

_____

_____

_____

_____

_____

_____

_____

_____

_____

_____

The major post–*The Proper Care and Feeding of Husbands* change another listener made was to stop the criticism. She realized that she was always correcting her husband because he did things in his own way, or because he had thoughts or ideas that were not always perfectly understandable to her—so she would voice her contrary opinion quite readily and loudly. Now she tries to keep her mouth shut when he would "be himself," and reports that he has been much more open and free to share his deeper emotions with her.

Ever wonder why your husband won't talk to you about his feelings? PROBABLY BECAUSE IT IS TOO DANGEROUS AND PAINFUL! I remember my years in private practice as a marriage and family therapist; women would complain that their men won't talk about their feelings, when the truth was that they only wanted their men to hear the wife's feelings—and be totally noncritical and totally supportive and in total agreement with whatever sentiment they were expressing. If the men dared to want to talk about their own feelings or voice opposition to hers, he was dead meat. Very motivating.

Your turn:

Think of some ways you could make your husband feel safer to discuss your issues and express his feelings—especially if they might be unpleasant for you to hear.

_____

_____

_____

_____

_____

_____

_____

_____

_____

It is so sad to hear from women that their men are not showing them love. However, when I do some detective work, I find that their men are doing all kinds of wonderful things for them. It's just that these "doings" don't seem to register on the woman as "love-speak." Men don't speak that much, they "do." "Doing" is the basic language of men. You are going to be an unhappy woman, with their love falling on deaf ears, if you don't accept that men express their love differently from women. As one woman offered, now she sees that *"He shows me every day how much I mean to him, and now, thanks to your book, I do the same."* And, my dear friends, if you as a woman acknowledge these love-deeds, they will multiply.

Your turn:

Please make a list of all those little, medium, and large things your husband does daily, probably to show you love—even if you never looked at it that way before.

_____

_____

_____

_____

"I SPEAK—YOU LISTEN . . . NOW WE'RE COMMUNICATING!

Do you really mean it when you say, "Honey, I wish you would talk to me"?

Denise recently called my show, angry and hurt, to tell me that her husband told her she hasn't been a very good wife in the past eight years. They've only been married eight years!

DENISE: Well, what he said is that he doesn't see any positive qualities in me as a wife.

DR. LAURA: What did he point out were the positive qualities of a good wife?

DENISE: Being kind. He told me that I'm not kind to him. Yelling. He said I yell at him and I nag him.

DR. LAURA: And that's true, isn't it?

DENISE: Yes.

DR. LAURA: Well then, he told you the truth.

DENISE: Well, I don't know what to do.

DR. LAURA: Well, be kinder, stop yelling and nagging.

DENISE: But he says that I've had no positive qualities since we've been married. That's not realistic.

DR. LAURA: Maybe so. But maybe it's hard to see your positive qualities when somebody is not kind and they're always yelling and nagging.

DENISE: OK.

DR. LAURA: So, if you get rid of the unkindnesses, the yelling, and the nagging, I guarantee you he'll see the other nice qualities. Let me ask you this question: If I

> took you outside of yourself and turned you into a
> man married to Denise, would you be happy?
> DENISE: *(sigh)* No, I guess not.
> DR. LAURA: Then behave in a way that would make you
> happy under that reversed circumstance.
> DENISE: OK, thank you.

Your turn:

Try Denise's exercise: if you were the man married to you—what would you
be happy about, and what would you not be happy about?

_____

_____

_____

_____

_____

_____

_____

_____

_____

After dinner one night, one of my listeners asked her husband if he was happy with her as his wife. Her heart beat faster
in anticipation of what he might say. It was at that point she
realized that she wasn't sure what she would hear. That made
her feel out of touch with his feelings—and she understand-
ably felt vulnerable.

His first response was to ask why she was asking. She told
him that she just wanted to know because his happiness was
important to her. He was probably worried that this was the
typical female trap of "Tell me anything bad and I'll make
your life a living hell."

He began by telling her all the wonderful things about her
and about how happy he truly was. He then continued . . . oh
my . . . to tell her of an area where her behavior could use
some improvement.

Instead of defensiveness and argument, she simply listened and then agreed with him that the issue was something she should and would work on.

He ended his response by telling her how much he loved her.

> *"Any wife who thinks there is no room for improvement is on the first step to apathy. Apathy could be the beginning of a downward spiral. I encourage any woman who is up for a challenge and a little vulnerability, to consider 'checking' in with her husband for a report card."*

And speaking about challenges, how 'bout all those mood swings? All premenopausal and perimenopausal women deal with mood swings of one degree or another. Those hormonal challenges often negatively impact our state of mind and our ability to be patient; we tend to be more emotional and reactive. We can get downright bitchy.

> *"I'm recognizing that my mood swings can make me get ugly, and I am reminding myself to let things roll off my back. What a big difference that makes!"*

Men have been at a big disadvantage here: If they say, "Oh, you're having your period," we get hostile with them for discounting our feelings or negating our argument; if they, however, don't show sensitivity to the fact we're having our period, we get hostile with them for not being considerate of our biology!

During our "hormonal challenges," we can:

- watch our diet
- take advantage of supplements that help with symptoms
- exercise more to increase our endorphins (happy brain chemicals)
- give everyone a heads up that today is a difficult day
- watch our mouth

Your turn:

Ask your husband for your report card: what he is happy about with respect to you, and what he would like you to change. Remember—don't ask for the truth if you're not going to handle the truth maturely, honorably, and lovingly. Truth is, you probably tell him about his C's, D's, and F's on a daily basis!

_____

_____

_____

_____

_____

_____

_____

_____

_____

_____

_____

Another reader got in touch with the typical female behavior of giving back to him your own interpretation of what he's said, and then proceeding to beat him over the head with how hurt you are . . . over your own interpretation of what he's said.

> *"I have often seen a look of shock, dismay, confusion and hurt on my husband's face as I give my own interpretation to something he's said. It breaks my heart to see that look when, if I am to be honest with myself, I know he meant no offense. In part of your book, you talk about women having to go over every detail of every word. It is very easy to confuse men."*

I think that this "translation" behavior on the part of us women is due to hypersensitivity and a defense mechanism to distract the discussion away from them and their uncomfortable comments. This listener found a way to handle her "urge" to do this behavior.

"We were driving in the car together yesterday. I put my hand on his leg (he was wearing shorts) and he said to me, 'Sweetie, your hands are freezing.'

"Well!!! A lightbulb went off over my head. Before your book, I would have either frozen him out or let loose with a spew of insults. Instead I said to him, 'Do you know what I just heard come out of your mouth? "Don't touch me!" "I don't love you," "I don't care about you," "You could freeze to death for all I care," "You are ugly and undesirable and I am sorry I ever met you!" '

"Well, after we both stopped laughing, he took my hand and said, 'Sweetie, your hands are freezing, let me warm them up for you.'

"I saw my husband's delight in my admission of my female, hypersensitive 'nuttiness' and my willingness not to deliberately misinterpret his intentions. *I HAD THE POWER TO MAKE EVERYTHING OK. I DID, AND IT WAS WONDERFUL!*"

Your turn:

Please review your memory banks for similar "interpretations." Think about what negative thoughts or worries this urge comes from. Try to follow the example above to make it different next time and record your experience.

_____

_____

_____

_____

_____

_____

_____

_____

_____

_____

One woman attached a poem she wrote to her husband the morning after reading *The Proper Care and Feeding of Husbands.*

> *"I dedicated this poem to my husband for our anniversary, which I blew off last week due to the smoldering feelings of resentment, bitterness, and general apathy I have held only for so long. You, Dr. Laura, have been able to transform the basic teachings in the Bible, which I often find so difficult to understand and implement in my life. I am forty-eight years old, and have often felt like it is too late for me to change the things that are passing me by both with my errors in marriage and as a mother.*
>
> *"But your simple and logical views have convinced me that it's never too late to become the sort of person I have been put on this great earth to be. I have been given the energy and desire to fulfill the purposes God had given me and that is starting with being a better wife and mother."*

I am including this poem as an example of deep, serious, meaningful communication between a hurting husband and his wife, who have gotten dangerously close to losing each other.

> *As I look back over the last nineteen years*
> *I find myself burdened with tears.*
> *Tears not of regret, anger, or feeling bad*
> *But of other things making me sad.*
>
> *Can you remember how we used to laugh and play?*
> *The things important then no longer seem to be today.*
> *What was once just you and me*
> *Is now smothered by "other" things we have to be.*
>
> *Gone seem to be the respect, love and romance*
> *Things we gave each other at every chance.*
> *Is now replaced with anger, bitterness, and selfish needs*
> *As well as disrespect, intolerance, and other weeds.*

How, we may ask, could this possibly be?
When just yesterday it seemed we were so free.
Freedom from stress, busyness and distractions
Seem to now be the main attractions.

What is important to me is not always for you
I have greatly failed to consider your point of view.
You are not a difficult creature to understand
I only needed to lend a helping hand.

How could I have missed something so simple yet pressing?
Why couldn't I see that you are God's blessing?
Instead I've whined, bitched, and complained
I've done all things from which I should have refrained.

How many times I've asked you to forgive
While all along I continue to relive.
All those heartless and selfish acts I commit
Not permanently changing myself one little bit.

I've made it too complicated and stressful for you to love
So now I have to turn it over to my Father above.
Only He can lead me down the right path
To become what you need and avoid further wrath.

I pray for His wisdom to show me how to love you
How to be supportive, patient, and respectful too.
But mostly I pray that He can soften your heart
So you can give me one last chance to try a new start.

Your turn:

Please write a poem to your husband, telling him what is on your mind and in your heart about your past and future lives together. Don't worry about rhyming.

_____

_____

_____

_____

_____

_____

_____

_____

_____

_____

_____

_____

_____

_____

_____

_____

_____

_____

_____

_____

_____

_____

MOMMY VS. WIFE IDENTITY CRISIS

At first thought, it is perfectly reasonable to imagine putting all your energy, time, attention, love, and affection into your children. I mean, aren't they cute, adorable, innocent, and totally dependent upon a mother for life itself, food, nurturing, protecting, and caretaking? Isn't it therefore obvious that everything else should be put aside to do that? Isn't it selfish to do otherwise? Isn't it selfish and immature for a husband to complain that he feels "on the outside," "ignored," "unimportant," "neglected," and like he's lost his girlfriend forever?

> *"My husband and I got to a place at which, after going round and round, rehashing the same old stuff, he told me he wanted a divorce—and he left. My world fell apart and I couldn't believe it! I cried and begged and pleaded with him, but it was no use. He had already seen a lawyer and suggested I do the same.*
>
> *"The next few days I was a mess. I thought about all I could have done differently and prayed my heart out for the strength to go on and be the best mom I could be. I would wake up with my then two-year-old, cherub-faced little boy in my bed next to me, and I would remember what had happened and would cry and cry.*
>
> *"I did everything you say in your book,* The Proper Care and Feeding of Husbands, *that I shouldn't have done. I had become totally consumed with being a mom. That's the ONLY thing that mattered to me. And when my husband would try to help, he never did it 'right,' so I would take over. I'd complain that he didn't help, then criticized when he did. I whined and complained about how he didn't spend enough time with us and I never appreciated how hard he worked so I could be my kid's mom."*

This reader and her family had just moved across the country, and because she was consumed with their son, she felt isolated and became needy—which, unfortunately, resulted in critical, demanding, perpetually angry behaviors. Her husband got to the point where he didn't want to come home, so he started working later and would go out with his boss for dinner and drinks—anything to avoid coming home to her.

Her mother, who had been an extremely negative person and wife, started poisoning her mind with thoughts of her husband's infidelity. However, when she would check up on him, he was exactly where he was supposed to be.

One night her husband called to ask if he could come over and spend time with their boy. She said yes and suggested she would leave and allow them time to themselves. He suggested she stay. She made his favorite meal. The next day he called and asked if she would like to go to the park and then out for dinner. They began courting all over again.

He moved back home two weeks after he'd left.

She started expressing her appreciation for him as a man and a husband.

> *"And I really did appreciate him . . . finally. He tried to explain to me one time before our near-divorce that he shows me he loves me by working hard and providing for our son and me. I hadn't seen it that way. I wanted more. But when I thought I had lost what I had for those two weeks after he left, I finally appreciated what I had."*

She now calls him at work, offers to get him lunch. She commends him. She supports him doing things with their son—without criticism. She asks for things without complaining about them. Basically,

> *"I am a wife again—not just a mommy. I let him know that he's my hero. And I get so much in return. More than I could ever imagine."*

Many other women have written to admit that they had completely immersed themselves in motherhood, very much to the exclusion of their husbands. When their men became distant, preoccupied, inattentive, uncooperative, unromantic . . . they blamed their men for being self-centered and didn't see their own contribution to the unhappiness in their homes.

How did one woman turn this all around?

> *"Your message, Dr. Laura, was loud and clear that I had been lacking in 'caring for' and 'feeding' my husband; the simple, loving gestures I gave so naturally years before and now showered only upon my daughter.*
>
> *"I gradually began showing him my appreciation and some*

kindness. When he would come into the room, I started getting up from whatever I was doing to hug and kiss him. I began smiling at him whenever I saw him. I started calling him during the day to tell him I'd been thinking of him. I would leave little love notes in his lunch box. I paid attention to the times when he needed me to pleasure him, rub his feet, massage his shoulders, and just be there for him.

"I thanked him for the things he would do. To my pleasant surprise, he began smiling and talking more openly. He's quick to help out in the kitchen now. And when I tell him about something around the house that broke or needs his attention, he is very willing to do whatever he can when he gets home from work.

"I now have the friend and lover back that I fell in love with so many years ago."

Many women actually believe they can have it all, and do it all well. Nope. One of those women wrote to me about her marriage problems. She knew she had placed him second or third in her priorities . . . but after all, they were married and shouldn't he just know she loves him? Shouldn't he just understand that she's busy? Shouldn't he just accept that things change as life goes on?

She had started accusing him of having an affair, because he wasn't talking to her about daily things and he wasn't initiating sex anymore.

He told her that he felt like they were just roommates and that he was lonely. She couldn't imagine how a guy in a nineteen-year marriage, with two teenage children, church, kids' sports, extended family, household chores, etc., could possibly be lonely?!

But, she realized, that was exactly the problem!

"I put all those things before my husband. He used to come to me at night to find a lover, but 90 percent of the time he found a tired, drained girl. I though I was a woman who could juggle

it all—how wrong I was. I was an immature, selfish female who had a very patient husband until he finally reached his limit.

"Because I neglected him for so long, he had developed a calloused heart toward me. He lost the butterflies and tingles and is not sure they'll return. I read so many letters in your book from husbands who are heartbroken because we women don't understand our men. Sex to guys is like talking is to gals.

"I hope my husband will give me another chance . . ."

It is too easy a trap to fall into; "ignore the husband because the kids need you more and he can take care of himself" trap. This sentiment only gets you an isolated, alienated, bitter, lonely, reciprocally unloving husband.

Your turn:

Please just brainstorm down all your daily/weekly activities in no particular order. Considering the amount of time allotted to each one, and the passion with which you approach it, go back and renumber them based on the priority you've given each. Where does your husband fit in?

_____

_____

_____

_____

_____

_____

_____

_____

_____

_____

Please ask your husband if anything—and, if so, what specifically—sometimes makes him feel lonely or alone in your family/marriage.

_____

_____

_____

_____

_____

_____

_____

_____

_____

   Please think about what you do to let your husband know you think about HIM on a daily/weekly basis.

_____

_____

_____

_____

_____

_____

_____

_____

_____

   What kinds of things do you do together during the month that mostly *you* like to do?

_____

_____

_____

_____

_____

_____

_____

_____

What kinds of things do you do together during the month that mostly *he* likes to do?

_____

_____

_____

_____

_____

_____

_____

_____

_____

_____

What kinds of things do you do together during the month that you both like to do?

_____

_____

_____

_____

_____

_____

_____

_____

_____

_____

What kinds of new things could you two do together?

_____

_____

_____

_____

BUT WHAT ABOUT WHEN I'M NOT IN
THE MOOD? . . .
THE "GETTING" IS IN THE "GIVING"!

This section is not only about sex, it is about all ways in which you may give and sacrifice your own immediate gratification for the gratification of your man.

Which is a far more "giving" act: to share a cookie when you have ten and have already eaten six or sharing a cookie when you only have one and you're hungry?

Of course it's easy to be loving and giving when you're filled up with energy and joy. The real measure of your love and commitment is demonstrated by your acceptance of the unique, sincere needs of your husband and your loving obligation to respond to his reasonable requests or desires with compassion and affection.

One reader wrote that she almost did not read my book because she is four months pregnant and already has a four-year-old and a two-year-old. She is spent! She thought, therefore, that she was entitled to not have to think about her husband's needs, because she is busy and hormonal.

> "But I knew deep down in my heart that the best time to take care of my husband was when I was going to need him the most. So even though I felt queasy, large, had heartburn, and was tired, I came to bed naked and ready.
>
> "So when women have been calling in to your show saying, 'But I don't feel like it,' laugh, Dr. Laura, because if a pregnant

mom of two who has spent part of the day vomiting can do it, they can, too! The result? I am enjoying it! The other night I kissed my husband good-night and he smelled like he did the other night when we made love. I felt my insides go all a-flutter. It was exciting—something I had not felt since early in the marriage or on vacation. What a thrill!"

Remember Mother Laura's prime directive: NEVER TURN DOWN A PERFECTLY GOOD ORGASM BECAUSE YOU'RE ANNOYED . . . OR MOODY!

"I used to be the kind of wife that thought of sex as something my husband earned for 'good behavior.' And that good behavior was defined by me. I would justify withholding sex because I was exhausted after a busy day of caring for my two young daughters and teaching piano students—as if my day was any more busy and demanding than his. If he was lucky or being unusually nice to me, I would 'give in' once in a while—when I felt like it.

"I am ashamedly guilty of telling my husband that after caring for everyone else's needs all day long, the last thing I wanted to do was another chore (sex) for him. At times, I would deliberately not participate, lying motionless and waiting for him to be done before sighing annoyedly and turning over to go to sleep without as much as a kiss.

"He told me that one of the most important things for him was to feel that I wanted him (another rolling of the eyes), and would talk jealously of friends' relationships if it was brought to light that the wife actually enjoyed and initiated sex.

"Then I read your book, The Proper Care and Feeding of Husbands. *With tears streaming down my face through much of it, I realized how destructive my behavior was to our marriage. I have implemented changes and I have to tell you, Dr. Laura, it is MAGIC! The feelings of love and respect for my husband have grown this past week, and I feel closer to him than at any other time in our eight-year marriage.*

"He is being more caring, more attentive, more fun . . . and

even ironed a shirt for me without being asked! I am truly amazed what a simple reminder of kindness, thoughtfulness, and selflessness can do for a marital relationship.

"Society teaches women to be aggressive, self-centered, and to be on constant lookout for 'me' time. Women have been misled under the guise of fighting oppression. Following the guidelines in your book have been truly liberating for me."

This letter is typical of the hundreds I have received expressing the concept of immediate gains. However, when we think of "getting," it usually suggests some "thing" that comes from another. That is shortsighted. Women who move past the ingrained notions that giving to a husband is giving up something of themselves, learn that instead of losing something, they feel a deep sense of gain.

The gain is a self-respect, an awe, and a wonderment that being a *woman* can be so important, benevolently powerful, special, sweet, mysterious, alluring, charming, seductive, flirtatious, needed, desired, respected, and so much more. What women "get" from "giving" to their men is an unbelievable new sense of purpose and meaning, a life that has far greater definition than one gotten from the feminist promise of female happiness.

What has been truly amazing is that in addition to women discovering the value of their womanliness, they have realized that their grateful husbands will give them the world—will cook, clean, wash, fix, and so forth—and never for a moment consider it demeaning or unmanly; men live to take care of their women—when their women appreciate them. Don't forget those A's from *The Proper Care and Feeding of Husbands:* attention, approval, appreciation, and affection. They are the keys to the kingdom.

Your turn:

Think about all the times you "weren't in the mood" for sexual intimacy or for going out to dinner without the kids, taking a shower together, hanging out with him, going somewhere only he is really interested in, and so forth. What do you think your rejection said to him?

_____

_____

_____

_____

_____

_____

_____

_____

_____

_____

Describe the times when you "did it" because you couldn't avoid " it"... however, once into "it," you discovered that you got with "it." What can you learn from that?

_____

_____

_____

_____

_____

_____

_____

_____

_____

Which of the two of you generally "decides" if sex is going to happen?

_____

_____

_____

_____

_____

_____

_____

_____

_____

_____

Do you think your husband has to "earn" sex? If so, how can he earn it—guaranteed!

_____

_____

_____

_____

_____

_____

_____

_____

_____

Please consider the license you give yourself to behave badly during emotional upsets, hormonal surges, and tough days. Imagine what it would be like to be on the receiving end of that. Would you like to come home to you?

_____

_____

_____

_____

_____

_____

_____

_____

_____

Think about the times you forced yourself to be nice to the mailman or your girlfriend—but wouldn't pull it together for your husband. Explain that.

_____

_____

_____

_____

_____

_____

_____

_____

Please consider the ways you may have avoided your "feminine powers" because of thinking they were manipulative, or degrading to yourself.

_____

_____

_____

_____

_____

_____

_____

_____

After reading *The Proper Care and Feeding of Husbands*, and getting this far in this workbook, please write about whatever changes you've made with respect to getting in touch with "your feminine side"!

_____

_____

_____

_____

_____

_____

_____

_____

And of course, there is the more standard concept of getting for giving:

> *"In short, your book has helped both of us to relearn how to be caring partners and do things for each other because we want to and love each other . . . not just because we're supposed to."*

And:

> *"About a week after I read your book, my husband put new tires on my car and spent two days putting a complete new air-conditioning system in it so I would be cool this summer—it's January! He also invited me to meet him for lunch the other day while the kids were in school. That's the first time he's done that in about two years!"*

Your turn:
Notice the difference in your husband's behavior since you read *The Proper Care and Feeding of Husbands* and made some changes. What have you noticed different in him?

_____

_____

_____

_____

_____

_____

_____

_____

ALL HE REALLY NEEDS IS YOU

My favorite letter best describing the concept "All He Really Needs Is You" comes from a woman who had gone to marital therapy to discuss why her husband sat in front of the TV with the remote day after day, was depressed, unhappy, didn't want to interact with the kids, etc.

Frustrated and feeling hopeless, she bought my book as a last resort in the hopes that she would learn why her marriage was so bad. It was the chapter on sex that struck her the most, especially the part that talked about how a man loves a woman no matter what she looks like . . . he's just happy to be with her. It finally struck her: she was fifty pounds overweight and embarrassed about how she looked.

"I blamed everyone but myself for my weight. I was always neat and clean but had always prided myself on being very good-looking and thin. I'm still good-looking, but Rubenesque now. Anyway, I took a risk.

"I pursued my husband with my chubby little body and he LOVED it. He didn't care a hoot what I looked like, and it was the best sex we have had in a long time. We started to giggle when the kids were around, and cuddled and spoke sweet nothings on the phone. The kids were giving us strange looks!

"Well, my husband has NEVER in twenty years bought me a piece of clothing. On our twenty-year anniversary he bought me a red thong from Victoria's Secret—and he selected it because it was too small and would show, you know, my private parts. He finds this very sexy and I never knew it.

"Anyway, when the kids were at school and I just walked in from working out, I said a quick hello and said I was going to take a shower. In his usual fashion, he grunted and never looked up. I squeezed myself into the little red thong, came downstairs wearing only the thong, and asked, 'Honey, does this make me look fat?'

"He looked at me and just stared. Then he smiled and said,

'Let's take a closer look upstairs.' Well, we were pretty busy for the next two hours.

"I am now getting rid of my shrink and spending my money at Victoria's Secret instead. My husband, my marriage, and my kids, and I thank you from the bottom of my thong!"

She didn't have to be perfect to be his dream lover. She just had to be willing to give herself to him with love, acceptance, openness, and a sense of humor.

Your turn:
Because of what characteristics of yours that you don't like do you keep part of yourself from your husband?

_____

_____

_____

_____

_____

_____

_____

_____

_____

Another wife feels she has become a better wife because of my radio program. Her husband is a bit of a perfectionist and gets down on himself when he makes mistakes when playing the guitar. If too many mistakes happen, he berates himself as being a worthless loser. In the past she would argue with him, and they would end up yelling at each other.

This time she did something different. When he said that he was going to smash the guitar or sell it, she pointed out that those weren't the only choices—and then she stopped talking. She made a written list of the twenty or so reasons he was lovable and simply handed him the list when he came out of his practice room feeling lousy.

After he read it, his whole manner changed, and he hugged her, saying what a wonderful thing she had done. He apologized for his behavior and made copies and posted them everywhere—to remind himself.

She didn't give him a good argument or a good talking-to about his immature behavior. She gave herself, her love, her respect, and her compassion; and he was healed.

Another wife wrote me that, based on my teachings, she greeted her *["completely devoted and underappreciated"]* husband with a cup of coffee and she looked into his eyes and told him how proud she was of him and how much she appreciated how hard he works.

His eyes immediately filled with tears. He folded her into his arms and said, "That's all I live for."

"That's all he lives for?!?! We've always been happily married, but we're going to be a whole lot happier from now on."

Another listener confirmed again the singular importance of you to your man. After her husband came home from a particularly stressful day, he played with the kids, talked, laughed, and had a great family evening. After the kids were asleep, they were cuddling on the couch when she said that she was sorry he had such a hard day, and hoped the next day would be better.

"He nuzzled his head in my shoulder and said, 'I'm fine now. I just wanted to come home to my family where I know I'm loved and accepted for who I am.'
"I was totally blown away!"

Finally, another listener sent me a copy of the letter her husband wrote her for Valentine's Day, after she made some attitude and behavior changes based on *The Proper Care and Feeding of Husbands:*

"Thank you for making me feel like a real man. I feel much more confidence in my daily routine and I feel invincible again.

Your ability to be able to change, with almost no bumps, shows true love. I love you more now than ever."

So, my dear friend, when some woman friend of yours asks with sarcasm why you build up your husband so, answer with, *"Because I love him."*

Your turn:

Please take the space below to explore the ways in which, you are now realizing, your husband simply needs "you" for his well-being and joy of life.

_____

_____

_____

_____

_____

_____

_____

_____

_____

_____

_____

_____

_____

_____

_____

_____

_____

_____

_____

_____

_____

_____

_____

Endnote

Please spend the next several weeks keeping a journal of your journey toward *WOMAN POWER*. Please feel free to fax me updates at (818) 461-5140!

I appreciate how much work you've put into this journey. I am impressed that you love your husband more than you hate to look at your pores in a 10X magnification mirror! I am humbled that you trusted me to be your guide. The point of this whole experience is for you to not reduce yourself to nanny, housekeeper, or employee. Never forget that you are a woman, and that being a woman is a special blessing. Your feminine touch, your intuition and sensitivity, your sensuality, your special nurturing warmth create and sustain life from the womb through eternity.

Never stop being your husband's girlfriend and lover; and you will have the best of him as a man.

—*Dr. Laura Schlessinger*